ACTING WITH RESPECT

A THEATER-BASED APPROACH TO CREATING A MORE DIVERSE, HARMONIOUS AND PROFITABLE WORKPLACE

BY GEOFFREY SCHEER
DRAMATIC SCRIPTS BY ART FEINGLASS
PROGRAM CREATED BY ART FEINGLASS

COVER ART BY JOHN CARTER WOLFE

*Acting with Respect: A Theater-Based Approach
to Creating a More Diverse, Harmonious and
Profitable Workplace*

Copyright © 2018 by Geoffrey Scheer. All rights reserved.

Dramatic scripts (excluding "Monday Repeat") written by Art Feinglass

Cover design by John C. Wolfe
Twitter/Instagram @jcwolfeart

This publication may not be reproduced in whole or in any part. It may not be transmitted in any form or means, electronic or mechanical, or stored in a retrieval system. There may be no mechanical copying, photocopying, recording or other reproduction wihout prior written consent of the author.

ISBN-13: 978-1987564686

To Art Feinglass, the founder of the feast

CONTENTS

Acknowledgements   7

Section I – Character   13

Section II – Plot   19

Scene 1
"Who's On the Team?"   21

Scene 2
"The Nephew"   33

Scene 3
"The Meeting"   41

Scene 4
"A Simple Compliment?"   53

Scene 5
"Asking for a Date"   58

Scene 6
"Turning the Tables   64

Scene 7
"Happy Hour"   67

Scene 8
"People Will Talk"   71

Scene 9
"Under Pressure"   79

Scene 10
"Roommate"   87

Scene 11
"Too Old"   95

Scene 12
"Wheelchair Bound"   101

Scene 13
"Not Invited"   109

Scene 14
"Monday Repeat" 115
Scene 15
"Just Jokes" 121
Scene 16
"Who Flies?" 127

Section III – Conclusion 133

ACKNOWLEDGEMENTS

This book is the product of my writing, but the ideas contained in it (along with the dramatic scripts) belong solely to Art Feinglass.

I first met Art in the summer of 2004. He had contacted me on the recommendation of a friend to ask if I would be interested in performing a few scenes for a corporate training seminar he was conducting. I was an actor at the time and was, as the euphemism goes, "between jobs," so I said sure. It sounded like a good way to make a few bucks while avoiding doing actual work (which was, to be candid, my primary goal when I decided to become an actor).

I learned my lines mostly by rote, not paying much attention to whatever else was going on in the scenes. After all, this wasn't a real play, right? I didn't need to delve into my character's backstory or motivation. I didn't need to think too much about my relationship to the other characters or how my journey fit within the bigger picture of the piece. I was a well-trained actor who was just lending my talents to corporate

America for the day so I could make a few bucks and keep my fridge stocked with beer and frozen pizza.

But as I sat through that first session and began to see how my part in the scene work fit into the larger context of the training program, I was riveted. Art would follow each of the scenes by doing some question and answer with the audience, and whenever possible he would throw a few questions at us actors as well, and we would have to improvise our responses while remaining in character. That alone was enough to keep me on my toes, but it was what happened next that really intrigued me. Art would tie together everything we had just done -- the scenes, the Q&A, the improv -- with statistical evidence and data that supported the point he was trying to get across. Much of the information he presented was brand new to me, and it made me realize that my role in the program had greater significance than merely parroting dialogue for a few dollars.

The presentation was very well put together and, in my opinion, highly effective. What really made an impression on me, however, was the content. I loved the idea of trying to promote diversity and prevent harassment. The fact that our client likely brought us in as a way of merely limiting their own liability didn't diminish the message for me. We may have been working for corporate America (the *enemy* in the eyes of a young actor), but we were on the side of the angels.

We did five 90-minute sessions that day, and any performer will tell you that a five show day takes a toll. Yet despite any physical or mental fatigue, I left the building feeling exhilarated. I actually found myself thinking, "Man, I wish I could just do *this* full-time." Expressing a thought like that would have gotten me kicked out of The Boston Conservatory of Music, Dance and Theatre.

Over the next several years, I was fortunate to help present this program many times with Art all over the country. It fell short of being a full-time gig, but it did become an important piece in my financial jigsaw puzzle. More than that, I loved doing it. I always felt a little thrill whenever I'd get an email from Art asking if I was available for another round of sessions.

As I got older and my personal circumstances started to change (I got married, had a kid), it became apparent that the life of an actor/director/playwright and whatever other titles I'd picked up along the way was no longer for me. What I wanted to do was start a company of my own, and I wanted that company to follow the same model as the one that Art had started. I toyed around with a number of ideas and even implemented one for a time, but nothing really grabbed hold. Then in the fall of 2016, the lightbulb went off. Art hadn't been pursuing clients for his training programs for several years, so I thought to myself, "Why am I trying to reinvent the wheel here? If Art's not actively running the business anymore, why not reach out to him and ask if *I* could start it back up and try my hand at running it?"

I typed up an email to him which sat in my drafts folder for about a month. I'm not sure which I was more afraid of -- that he would say no and be offended that I'd asked, or that he'd say yes and I'd actually have to make this thing work.

Eventually I did hit send, and a couple days later he wrote me back to say he found my idea "intriguing" and that he'd be open to discussing it further. By the time we spoke on the phone the following week, he'd gone from intrigued to solidly on board. And thus the journey began.

Gratitude isn't a strong enough word to express my feelings for Art putting his program in my hands. Throughout this whole process, he has acted as cheerleader, consultant, therapist and surrogate father to me. He's trusted me with his legacy, cheered me through every success and encouraged me when I've been down. He's given me a second career and a renewed sense of purpose.

I owe him more than I could ever repay and I am forever grateful.

***

I've taken the point of view of analyzing workplace behavior using the same techniques I would use to analyze a character in a play. In adopting this approach, I have to acknowledge my debt to another influential figure in my life -- Steve McConnell, drama professor at The Boston Conservatory. Steve (as we were encouraged to call him) shaped my artistic sensibilities more than anyone, and his fingerprints are all over this book.

That said, there's a certain irony in recognizing Steve's impact on me as an artist as he would be the first to point out that the inclusion of drama in these training programs isn't art. Technically speaking, it's propaganda. Art is meant purely to be observed, not to serve any practical purpose nor to advance an agenda. And he'd be right. In this context, the use of drama *is* propaganda. I believe I'm on the right side of the issues I'm addressing, but in the strictest sense, propaganda is the correct term.

So *why* I'm using drama takes it out of the realm of being art. But *how* I use drama -- the craft involved -- stems from the lessons I learned from him all those years ago, and I couldn't have written this book without him. He gets my gratitude whether he likes it or not.

***

Finally, I would like to recognize all of the amazing Human Resource professionals and business leaders I've met and spoken with over the years. During the past two years in particular, I have travelled the country doing this presentation at conferences and chapter meetings for many business organizations, particularly those affiliated with the Society for Human Resource Management (SHRM). Following many of these presentations, I've had the opportunity to speak candidly with some of the attendees to find out what's happening on the front lines. Their willingness to share their experiences and expertise has given me an invaluable window into the challenges that companies of all sizes face, as well as some great tools to overcome those challenges. This book would not have been possible without their insight.

I
CHARACTER

One of the first things you learn in drama school is that there are no villains. At least, not in a play.

There may be characters that audiences think of as villains. There may even be characters drawn from real life whom history has determined to *be* villains. But as an actor who must inhabit a nefarious role, you can't look at your character and think of that person as evil. You aren't afforded the luxury of judgement.

If I were asked to play Hitler, I couldn't approach the character as if he were a villain, and for one simple reason -- because Hitler didn't think of himself as a villain. No one does. Nobody sees themselves that way. We all see ourselves as the heroes of our own stories. We may see ourselves as *flawed* heroes sometimes, but heroes nonetheless. Even when we do something that we know is wrong, or that later in life we come to regret, we don't think that in those moments we "turned villainous." We think about the situation and the particular circumstances that led us to behave -- *in that moment* -- in a way that was less than our heroic selves. But over the long arc of our lives, we still retain our hero status.

This is something we forget when others behave in ways that are contrary to our values. We immediately look at them and say, "Those are bad people. They and I are on opposite sides." We pass judgement, wall ourselves off and stand in our separate ideological corners. We don't stop to think that those people might be behaving in ways that they *honestly believe* are in the best interests of themselves and those around them.

There are, of course, extreme circumstances. People who are truly deranged -- mass murderers, serial rapists, sexual predators, anyone who would molest or otherwise prey on children -- belong in an entirely separate category. Analyzing their behavior is beyond my capabilities and outside the scope of this book.

The vast majority of us, however, make our way through this jumble of a thing called life doing what we think is right, or at the very least, what we *hope* is right. But we also have to balance doing what's right with trying to get what we want and what we hope will make us happy. And sometimes, in that "pursuit of happiness," we don't fully consider how our actions might affect those in our orbit. Sometimes we don't realize the profound impact that an offhand remark can have on somebody. Other times, we weigh the importance of the thing we want against the hurt we could potentially inflict on another person and decide that the balance is in our favor. The path between self-interest and empathy is a narrow one, and we all have blind spots.

In the workplace, minor offenses -- intended or otherwise -- can be magnified dramatically. The workplace is a "small world" type of environment, and unlike other relationships in our lives, we don't usually have the option of avoiding our co-workers or severing ties with them completely. Get into a tiff with your spouse and you can give each other the silent treatment for a few days. Your mom said something over the phone that touched a nerve? Looks like her calls won't be getting returned for a while. But the co-worker you offended on Monday becomes your project partner on Wednesday, and the workday stops for no one. It can get complicated.

So how do we avoid the snubs, slights and slanders that set co-workers against each other and disrupt office harmony? I guess the short answer is that you can't, at least not entirely. The workplace is not a colony of insects, operating together as a hive. It's a collection of individuals, each with their own opinions, flaws and unique points of view. And the more diverse your workforce, the greater potential for misunderstandings (though there's also enormous benefit to a diverse workforce, as I'll illustrate throughout the book). But if we can remember that everyone we interact with is seeing the world through the filter of their own experience -- and typically behaving in a way that they believe is right and justified -- then maybe we can be a little less quick to judge and to distance ourselves. Maybe we can cultivate a greater sense of empathy. Maybe we can find it just a bit easier to accept people for who they are, to understand where they're coming from and to open a dialogue with them. If we can do that, there's a better chance that they'll be able to understand and empathize with *us*.

As a former actor, director and playwright, I have come to fully accept and believe in the notion that there are no villains in theater, but I still struggle with the idea that there are no villains in the world. It's been said that a villain is just the hero of the other side, and I suppose that's true. However, that doesn't make it easy for me to accept or fully understand the viewpoints of those who I believe are on the wrong side of an issue (and God knows that the echo chamber of social media is not making things easier). I know that I'm imperfect, that I can rush to judgment and slam the door on my fellow human beings as quickly as the next person. I'm trying to do better, but like everyone else, I'm a work in progress.

I like to think that if I could approach the world with the same kind of dispassionate professionalism with which I approach a character in a play, I would be a much more forgiving person. And this is, in fact, precisely the approach I take in the training seminars I conduct all around the country. I bring in actors, have them play out scenarios that could land their characters in trouble in the workplace, and then ask the audience to figure out, not who was wrong and who was right, but *why* these characters behaved the way they did, and how their actions affected the other characters in the scene.

Throughout the course of this book, I'll use the same dramatic format to investigate a host of issues including discrimination, harassment and sometimes just plain, old-fashioned misunderstanding. As the reader, you will have to put on your acting hat and see if you can look at each character from his or her own perspective and find a way to justify their actions.

The goal here is not to provide a list of dos and don'ts for office behavior (most people, myself included, don't like being told what they can and can't do). The goal is to try not to judge these characters, regardless of what our initial reactions to their behavior might be. We are attempting to, as Shakespeare said, "hold the mirror up to nature," and demonstrate that we are all wonderfully flawed human beings trying to make it through the day -- and usually, most of the time, trying to do what's right.

Do we fall short sometimes? Absolutely. But those are typically failures of vision or judgement, not failures in character.

For the purposes of this book, we're going to work off of the premise that -- extreme circumstances aside -- in life, just as in a play, there are no villains. If we can do that, maybe we can begin to move toward a workplace culture where everyone feels respected, valued and safe.

II
PLOT

Scene 1

"Who's On the Team?"

Imagine the following scenario: George, a midlevel manager in his late 30's, has been asked to spearhead a new project. His first task is to assemble a team from among the various departments in the office. He enlists the help of Marie and Carol, two of his direct reports, and the three of them begin putting a group together.

The deadline to finalize the team is fast approaching, but they are still one member short. George is dragging his feet, unable to commit to anyone. Eager to help him make a decision, Marie and Carol get together and come up with a list of four highly qualified candidates for the open position. They bring this list to George in his office.

MARIE. George, this can't wait any longer. You have to pick one more person for the project team.

GEORGE. Okay. Who have you got?

MARIE. How about Charlotte?

GEORGE. Charlotte's good. She's smart, hard working ... wait. Isn't she the one with the young kids? What if she has to leave a meeting early because one of her kids gets sick?

CAROL. All kids get sick once in a while, George. That's not a big deal.

GEORGE. Yeah, but it means you can't count on her to be at the job when you need her. Nah. Who else?

MARIE. What about Charlie?

GEORGE. Charlie's a little *old*, don't you think? Are we sure he's gonna have the energy for this? Hell, he'll probably *die* halfway through the project.

CAROL. You're really terrible. Okay, how about Singh? He's young, energetic, he's not planning to die anytime soon ...

GEORGE. Singh's good ... but he's got that *accent*. That'd really foul things up. Nah. Who else you got?

CAROL. How about Harry?

GEORGE. Umm ... Harry's a little ... "light in the loafers," if you know what I mean. The other guys wouldn't be comfortable working with him.

MARIE. Okay, George. Let me get this straight. You don't want Charlotte because she's a working mother.

GEORGE. Can't count on her.

MARIE. You don't want Charlie because you think he's too old.

GEORGE. Over the hill!

MARIE. You don't want Singh because he has an accent.

GEORGE. Won't be able to understand him.

MARIE. And you don't want Harry because you think he might be gay.

GEORGE. "Might" be gay?

CAROL. So, George, who are you going to put on the team?

GEORGE (*honestly puzzled*). I have no idea. You know what this company *really* needs? More people like *me!*

***

What do we think of George? Most people, I imagine, have a pretty low opinion of him at this point, and understandably so. In the course of a brief scene, he's managed to make disparaging comments about working mothers, the elderly, people from other countries and the LGBTQ community. It would be pretty easy to view him as a monster.

But what if you were the actor who had to play him? What if you had to *become* George, see the world through his eyes and justify the lines you were asked to deliver?

At this point, I feel it's necessary to take a quick sidebar and talk about how an actor prepares for a scene. Contrary to popular opinion, most actors don't spend hours on end conjuring up memories of their dead dog in order to whip themselves into an emotional frenzy. Instead, they ask a few basic questions, the most important of which being, what does my character want? What is my *objective* in the scene? What is it I'm trying to get, and who am I trying to get it from? What is my relationship to that person?

The next question is what (or who) is preventing me from getting what I want? What's standing in my way? What is the *obstacle*?

Finally, what sorts of actions will I take to overcome the obstacle(s) in order to achieve my objective? What *tactics* will I employ?

Objectives, obstacles and tactics. Remember these terms.

Swinging our focus back to the scene, what is it that George wants? What is his objective? Is it to offend Carol and Marie? To sabotage the project? To get reported to HR and lose his job? (If so, he's on the right track!)

While any of those objectives might be fun to play around with, it seems clear from the script that what George really wants is to pick the best person for the team. His intention here, broken down to its simplest form, is actually noble. From his point of view, he honestly believes he is acting in the best interests of himself, his team and his company.

This brings us to our obstacle. In George's mind, the obstacle to getting what he wants is that he doesn't have the right people to choose from. In reality, the obstacle here is George himself. George is getting in his own way by thinking in stereotypes.

In drama, and in life, there is usually more than one obstacle standing in the way of us getting what we want. For every *external* obstacle we face, there is almost always an *internal* one as well. A baseball player looking to score the game-winning run with two out in the bottom of the ninth not only has to face the opposing pitcher (the external obstacle), but his own fear, nervousness and anxiety (internal obstacles) as well.

Those internal obstacles are often the most difficult for us to overcome since there is so much emotion involved. For instance, the man at bat may have faced this situation before and come up short. He could be asking himself, "Am I really up to this challenge, or will history repeat itself? The fate of the season -- and possibly my career -- is at stake. What happens if I fail?" If our hero is to have any chance of besting his rival, he will first need to face down his inner demons.

In George's case, overcoming *his* internal obstacle -- his penchant for thinking in stereotypes -- is particularly tricky because *he doesn't realize the obstacle is there*. It's practically impossible to solve a problem if you don't know it exists. And why does George have this blindspot? Why does he think the way he does, and how can he not see that this type of thinking is now holding him back?

Given the information we have from the scene, we can't know the answers to these questions with any certainty, but we can infer several possible *backstories*. One thing worth noting is that, in performance, George is always played by a white male. So perhaps we can assume that he didn't grow up in a particularly diverse environment. Maybe he's a "victim" of his own privilege. As a young, heterosexual, white collar, white male, he's probably never had to face the challenges that women and minorities face and is unable to envision the world from their points of view.

It might be hard to work up any sympathy for George here, particularly if you *are* a woman or a minority and have had to deal with some of the Georges of the world, and maybe sympathy isn't what we should be after anyway. But if we can understand why George is the way he is -- without condoning or excusing -- we can begin to find a way to address the problem and come to a solution.

Let's turn our focus for the moment to Carol and Marie. What do they want in this scene? What are their objectives?

In a general sense, they also want what George wants -- to pick the best person for the team. Ultimately, however, George is the one who has to make that choice, so specifically for this situation, I think we have to say that what Marie and Carol want is to guide George to a good decision.

In this task, they face the same obstacle that George does -- George's inability to think beyond stereotypes. The difference, of course, is that Carol and Marie are actually aware of the obstacle, and are therefore able to employ a couple of tactics as they attempt to achieve their goal.

After George has dismissed all of the potential candidates, Marie attempts to subtly shame George by reiterating all of the inappropriate things he's just said. Her hope seems to be that George will hear how ridiculous he sounds and realize how flawed his logic is.

Unfortunately for Marie, George is not a guy who gets subtlety.

Carol then makes a last ditch effort to save the situation by impressing upon George the difficulty of the corner he's just backed himself into. *If not these people, then who? We're running out of options!*

Sadly, this only sparks a response from George that further illustrates how blind he is to the problem. *If only everyone were more like me.* Then *we'd have a strong workforce!*

Another obstacle that Marie and Carol face here is the nature of their relationship to George. In every relationship, there is the issue of *status*. One person has upper status, one person has lower status. The degree of separation between upper and lower status is fluid depending on the relationship and the given circumstances, but it's there.

In the workplace, the people in charge almost always have upper status. They're the ones who decide who gets a raise and who doesn't; who lands a promotion and who gets left behind; who to hire and who to fire. This makes the situation for Carol and Marie that much more delicate. They might be *dying* to tell George that he's a sexist, racist, homophobic pig, but you can't say that to the boss. You have to keep your emotions in check and find another avenue.

So what could Marie and Carol do in this situation? How could they overcome their obstacles and achieve their objective of helping George choose the best candidate? What would *you* do in their place?

Right now, some of you may be thinking that it's time to take a trip to HR, and you may be right. But let's assume for the moment that Carol and Marie don't want to take that step just yet (we'll call that the "nuclear option"). What else could they do to help George get past thinking in stereotypes?

To my mind, they've got two courses of action that would be most effective. The first course is to counter George's stereotypes with facts.

Let's look at Charlotte, the first candidate for the team. If you go back and look at the scene, you'll notice that George never says Charlotte has a *track record* of missing meetings because of her kids. He expresses reservations that she might, in some hypothetical future, be forced to miss a meeting if one of her children becomes ill. He's projecting a stereotype of working mothers being unreliable because of their role as parents. But is that the situation here? Marie should ask George when, specifically, he remembers Charlotte having to miss an important meeting due to her kids. If George can't provide any specific examples (and if there's nothing in Charlotte's performance reviews to suggest she's unreliable), then Marie has just invalidated his argument, and done so in a way that does not betray the status of the manager/subordinate relationship.

What about Charlie? George's argument is that Charlie is too old to be a vital member of the team, that he lacks energy, that he may actually *die* if forced to exert himself.

Has Charlie lost a step? Have co-workers complained that he can't keep up or have managers noted a loss of vitality in his performance reviews? Has Charlie ever, in fact, collapsed in a heap and died in the middle of an important project?

If the answer to these questions is "no," you have again invalidated George's argument.

The best way to counter a stereotype is with facts. That said, there are, unfortunately, some people in this world who seem impervious to facts. Their brains are so hard-wired to believe in preconceived notions that they are unable to process new information, at least at first. But if you continue to chip away, force them to justify their beliefs and expose the flaws in their reasoning, there is always hope that they might come around.

The second course of action -- and the one that I think is most effective -- would be to bring these candidates in for a face to face meeting with George.

I think that something remarkable happens when we meet with a person face to face. It becomes much harder to deny someone's humanity when that person is standing right in front of you. At that moment, they're no longer an idea in your head or a caricature of real person. They are a living, breathing, flesh and blood human being, as unique, as flawed and as deserving of respect as you are. I have seen the walls of stereotypes break down for no other reason than two people simply sat in a room together and talked. I imagine we've all seen it happen at some point.

This country is more polarized than I can remember at any point in my forty plus years on this earth, and I am absolutely convinced that smartphones and social media play an outsized role in this. For all the "connection" these devices and platforms promise, we are losing honest, face to face, human interaction. We're hunkering down in our ideological hideouts and refusing to budge against people we increasingly see as enemies.

It is, of course, natural that we should gravitate towards people with whom we share common beliefs, values and backgrounds. We're at ease with these people. It's less challenging. It's also tempting to think, as George does, that the workplace would be better if everyone were like-minded and of similar upbringing. This would, one might surmise, limit misunderstanding and conflict, and allow the office to run more smoothly. And the smoother things run, the more productive -- and ultimately profitable -- the workplace should be. Right?

This seems to be exactly the argument that George is making. Unfortunately for him, evidence does not support this line of thinking.

Several years ago, Covenant Investment Management did a study of the S&P 500, rating them on their track record and openness in regard to hiring and promoting women and minorities. What they found was instructive. The one hundred companies that received the worst ratings -- that were *least* open to hiring and promoting women and minorities -- had an average return on investment of 7.9% The companies rated in the top 100 had an average ROI of 18.3%.

Simply put, companies that were more open to diversity were more than *twice* as profitable. (A study commissioned by Deloitte yielded nearly identical results.)

A more recent study by the consulting firm McKinsey & Company further reinforces those findings. Looking at 350 of the top companies in the U.S., Latin America and the U.K., they found that for every 10% improvement in diversity, there was a 2-4% increase in profitability.

The point here is not to get bogged down in a lot of numbers and statistics (I specifically went into the arts to avoid such things). The point is to demonstrate that companies do better when they are more diverse and inclusive.

Think of any movie where a ragtag group of misfits has to come together as a team to overcome great obstacles (sports and superhero movies come to mind). When joined together, the individual quirks that first seem like liabilities ultimately become the team's greatest assets. I think that these stories resonate because we've all witnessed some small version of this phenomenon in our own lives.

In my work as a playwright, I never cease to be amazed at what an actor can bring to one of my scripts. I've witnessed actors take lines I originally envisioned as dramatic and find moments of humor I hadn't realized were there -- and get the biggest laughs of the show! Other times, these artists have found unexpected poignancy in places I didn't intend, and the play ended up becoming richer than I could ever have imagined. And to think, if I had brought in actors who were too much like me, and who would have delivered those lines exactly as I heard them in my head, I would have lost all of those exquisite moments.

A company functions in the same way. We all bring our unique experiences into our jobs, as well as our quirks and idiosyncrasies. But when we are in an environment where we feel respected, valued and safe; where we are given a chance to contribute based on our strengths; and where we are embraced, not in spite of our differences, but because of them, then we have all the ingredients for a stronger, more engaged and ultimately more productive workforce.

It may well be that the very diversity we are so often afraid of is precisely what's needed in order to overcome the obstacles we face.

Scene 2

"The Nephew"

Let's delve a little deeper into the issue of diversity. In this scene, Carol is the Director of Sales. She is in the process of hiring an entry-level salesperson when she gets an unexpected visitor.

STEVE (*entering CAROL's office*). Hello, Carol.

CAROL. Steve, hello. What can I do for the Vice President of Sales today?

STEVE. Well, I wanted to talk to you about that entry-level sales position we've been looking to fill.

CAROL. Say no more. I think I've got the perfect candidate for us.

STEVE. Oh?

CAROL. I just finished the final interview with her this morning.

STEVE. Was that the young, African-American woman I saw leaving your office?

CAROL Yes it was. She's smart, motivated and she's got the right education and experience. She's just what we've been looking for.

STEVE. Actually, I had a suggestion.

CAROL. A suggestion?

STEVE. Nice young man. Very personable.

CAROL. Okay. What are his qualifications?

STEVE. Well, he doesn't look all that impressive on paper.

CAROL. How about his experience.

STEVE. No experience.

CAROL. I'm not sure I understand.

STEVE. This young man is the nephew of the Vice President of Marketing. He and I play golf together and he asked me if we could find a place for his nephew.

CAROL. But you say this kid has no qualifications.

STEVE. No, but he has a nice appearance. Looks like that actor, uh ... Zac Efron. You can teach him what he needs to know to get started.

CAROL. I don't know, Steve. I mean, we *just* got a memo regarding the company's hiring policies. It stressed the importance of hiring the most qualified candidate regardless of age, sex, national ori--

STEVE (*cutting her off*). Oh, yes. I read that memo. *Very* interesting.

CAROL. And yet you're asking me to hire some unqualified *nephew* over a highly qualified candidate?

STEVE. Whoa, whoa, whoa. I didn't say that. I just said I'd like you to ... *consider* him for the position.

CAROL. "Consider" him?

STEVE (*leaning closer to her for effect*). It would mean a lot to the VP of Marketing.

CAROL. And to you, I suppose.

STEVE. And to me.

(*Pause.*)

CAROL. I don't know, Steve.

STEVE (*breaking off and looking at his watch*). Ooh, I've got to get to a meeting. It's been nice chatting with you, Carol. (*Pointedly*) I know you'll do the right thing.

(*STEVE exits.*)

CAROL (*to herself*). Hire the best candidate or advance my career? Commitment to promoting diversity or commitment to *being* promoted? Do the right thing or keep paying my mortgage? What am I gonna do?

***

What *is* Carol going to do? What *should* she do?

In a hypothetical situation such as this, the answer seems perfectly clear -- Carol should hire the qualified candidate. But in life, it's not always so easy.

We went over the issue of status in the previous scene, and here it plays a central role. All things being equal, hiring the most qualified candidate is both the right thing to do and the smart thing to do. But things are not equal in this situation. Steve -- a Vice President in Carol's department who holds considerable power over her -- has strongly suggested that she hire the nephew of another powerful person in the company. Even with company policy on her side, that's a huge obstacle to overcome. Or as a person at one of my sessions once put it, "I'm not sure who *should* get the job, but I know who *will*."

Let's take a look at Steve's motivation. Does he want to quash the hiring of the other candidate because that person is a woman and a minority? It's hard to tell going off of the limited information we're provided in the scene (the *given circumstances*), although he does appear dismissive of the memo that sets out the company's commitment to diversity. It's possible that a certain amount of bias towards women and minorities plays a role in his thinking, but we can't say for sure. What we can say, given what we know, is that he's not really concerned with promoting diversity or hiring based on qualifications. Steve wants to do a favor for his golfing buddy in marketing, and his intention in this scene is to coerce Carol into hiring the nephew.

So, is there any argument to be made for Carol hiring the nephew? This is a question I always put to the audience in my training sessions, and I've been amazed over the years at the number of times people have argued yes, she should hire the nephew. These folks recognize that there are times you have to do what the boss tells you to do (or asks you to "consider" doing), even if you know it's wrong. Sometimes things just boil down to a matter of survival. Though with that said, hiring the nephew may not ensure Carol's survival at all. As another astute member of my audience once pointed out, if Carol *hires* the nephew she may be the one who ultimately has to *fire* the nephew if and when he proves to be incompetent. Then she'll *really* be in hot water.

Maybe we can't blame Steve for wanting to help out a friend, but we can certainly label him as shortsighted (if nothing else). By pushing the nephew onto the payroll, he's putting his department in a terrible position. He's forcing a weak hire onto the team and robbing the organization of a chance to become more diverse in the process. It's also possible that Steve may indeed be biased against the minority candidate but entirely unaware of it. His actions may be a result of unconscious bias.

Women and minorities are still underrepresented in many top industries, and there's a good argument to be made that unconscious bias in the hiring process is the root cause. In 2004, a landmark study published in the American Economic Review showed that job applicants whose resumes listed an African-American sounding name were 50% *less likely* to be granted an interview than candidates who had white sounding names, despite their resumes being nearly identical. Those findings have been challenged over the years by some who argue that other factors such as socioeconomic status play an outsize role, but by and large the study has held up.

Another interesting case is that of the Toronto Symphony Orchestra. Back in the 1970s, the TSO came under scrutiny for its lack of diversity as every single one of its musicians were white males. Leaders of the orchestra bristled at the notion that race or gender played a role in their hiring decisions. They firmly believed they were hiring the best people based solely on talent and ability. Yet they couldn't deny the incongruity of the notion that only white men could live up to that musical standard.

What the TSO decided to do became a kind of social experiment. They began holding blind auditions. A screen was set up on the stage so the auditioners couldn't see who was playing. Musicians were assigned a number and instructed not to speak or do anything that might give away their gender, ethnicity, age or any other personal information. They just played. The result? Within a couple of seasons, the orchestra became nearly evenly split between men and women, with a marked increase in minority musicians as well.

Several major companies have adopted a similar principle, initiating what's known as "blind recruitment." In this practice, information such as age, name and gender are removed from an applicant's resume. Deloitte, HSBC and the BBC have all recently implemented this strategy, though it's too early to tell what effect it's had.

These examples touch on efforts to mitigate the effects of unconscious bias, which we'll discuss in even greater detail in the next chapter. The situation in our scene between Steve and Carol has more to do with direct pressure against hiring a minority candidate. For a real life example of this scenario, we turn to the case of Harvey C. Russell.

Mr. Russell began working for the Pepsi-Cola Company in 1950 as a field representative, where his job was to help move the product into so-called "ethnic markets." He worked his way up the company ladder throughout the decade, and in 1962, Pepsi became the first major American company to appoint an African-American to the position of Vice President by promoting Mr. Russell to VP of Special Markets.

To say that the news was not well met by everyone would be an understatement. In fact, the Ku Klux Klan -- a much more influential organization at the time -- called for a nationwide boycott of all Pepsi products, and Pepsi's sales plummeted.

This was two years before the Civil Rights Act of 1964. Jim Crow was still the law of the land in many parts of the country, and Pepsi, though a big company, was not nearly the size or stature that it is today. Back then, Coke was the good stuff you served to your guests in the living room. Pepsi was the cheap stuff you drank with your family in the kitchen. Many inside the company feared that they would not be able to weather the financial storm.

You can imagine the considerable pressure Pepsi would have been under from shareholders and other interested parties to remove Mr. Russell from his position. But Pepsi believed that they had the right man, so they stuck to their guns, not just keeping Mr. Russell on, but appointing him to an even more powerful position three years later as the VP of Corporate Planning.

Currently, PepsiCo is ranked number 44 on the Fortune 500 and has been ranked by The Ethisphere Institute -- a business ethics watchdog -- as one of the most ethical companies to work for in the U.S. for twelve years running.

Promoting diversity in the workplace isn't always easy. Oftentimes it requires overcoming both internal obstacles (unconscious bias) and external ones (pressure to hire non-diverse candidates). But it is the right thing to do and the smart thing to do. If you're able to keep your eye on the bigger picture, you may find substantial rewards down the road.

Scene 3

"The Meeting"

The next few chapters will look at issues that affect women in the workplace. In our first example, George is the VP of Sales. He is leading a meeting with two of his managers, Steve and Marie.

STEVE. So, to sum up, I think the facts as I've presented them really do justify the proposed strategy.

GEORGE. Excellent report, Steve. You've obviously done your homework.

STEVE. Thank you, George.

GEORGE (*looking at his agenda*). All right. Next up is a report from ... (*GEORGE looks up at MARIE and takes note of the outfit she's wearing.*) Ah! "Pretty in pink" Marie.

(*MARIE is clearly annoyed by the comment but decides to brush it off.*)

MARIE (*referring to her notes*). Test market results have been very encouraging. In the Philadelphia area, sales are up 12%.

(*MARIE looks up from her notes to gauge GEORGE's reaction only to find that he and STEVE have taken out their smartphones and are scrolling through them.*)

MARIE. Um ... we encountered some initial consumer resistance, but we were able to get past that. Our team worked very hard, and it's paid off.

(*GEORGE waves to STEVE and indicates that he's going to send him a text.*)

MARIE. Total market share increased to 28%.

(*GEORGE and STEVE share a laugh at what's on their phones.*)

MARIE. So, I don't know if this is too bold, but I was thinking we could roll out the program and test market in other areas around the country.

(*GEORGE and STEVE continue to ignore her.*)

MARIE. To get a good cross section of reaction nationwide, I was considering Seattle, Kansas City and Savannah.

(*There is a long pause. Finally, GEORGE realizes that MARIE has finished her presentation.*)

GEORGE. Oh! Uh ... thank you, Marie. Very nice report.

STEVE. Yes. Nice report, Marie. Hey, George?

GEORGE. Yeah?

STEVE. I just had an idea. What if we roll out the program and test market in a few select cities around the country?

GEORGE (*intrigued*). Around the country?

STEVE. Say, just off the top of my head, Seattle, Kansas City, maybe Savannah?

(*MARIE's mouth drops to the floor. GEORGE ponders the idea for a moment.*)

GEORGE. Hmm ... I like it. Good thinking, Steve!

STEVE. Thank you, George.

MARIE. Yeah. Good thinking, *Steve*.

STEVE. Thank *you*, Marie.

GEORGE. Okay, I see it's almost time for lunch. Why don't we adjourn a little early? We'll meet back here at 2:00.

STEVE. Sounds good.

GEORGE. Hey, Steve. You got a minute?

STEVE. For you, George? Always.

GEORGE (*crossing to STEVE*). Why don't you join me for lunch? I want to talk to you about that new project in *Paris*.

STEVE (*standing*). Paris? I *love* Paris!

(*MARIE watches as the two men exit.*)

MARIE (*to no one in particular*). Thanks, guys. I'd love to join you for lunch. Thanks for asking.

***

So ... how did that meeting go for Marie? Not so great, right? Did the situation depicted seem realistic? That most likely depends on your experience, point of view and one other notable (and crucial) factor.

In September of 2017, after a conversation with a friend, astronomer Nicole Gugliucci took to twitter to coin a new term -- "hepeating." In Dr. Gugliucci's words, *hepeating* is "when a woman suggests an idea and it's ignored, but then a guy says the same thing and everyone loves it."

Within days of Dr. Gugliucci's tweet, the term #hepeated had been re-tweeted over 65,000 times, and within a few weeks, articles addressing the phenomenon appeared in Business Insider, Huffington Post, CNBC and scores of other online news and media sites.

Whenever I bring up this phenomenon in my presentations (which I was doing long before there was a word to define it) I am always struck by the reactions I get from the audience. The men will look at me with blank stares as if to say, "What on earth are you talking about? I've never heard of this happening (much less been a party to it) in my life!"

Simultaneously, the women will all be nodding their heads up and down in furious recognition and agreement.

Clearly there's a disconnect.

In our first scene, George was completely unaware that he was thinking of the people around him as stereotypes rather than fully developed, three-dimensional human beings. In this scene, we see that same lack of self-awareness, with both George and Steve exhibiting an unconscious bias toward Marie.

Unconscious bias can be a tricky thing to portray as an actor because it's inactive, and you can't *play* something that isn't an action. Instead, you have to play your intention in the scene with full commitment and make a conscious effort to disregard what you, the actor, know is *really* going on underneath. When playing George or Steve, you don't tell yourself you're actively ignoring Marie because she's a woman. You think, "I'm shifting my focus to something more deserving of attention given the current circumstances of the meeting." That can be a stretch for the actor who is fully aware of just how terribly George and Steve are behaving toward Marie -- and may have strong personal feelings about it -- but sometimes that's the actor's job.

In life, unconscious bias is tricky because we have literally no idea we hold these biases and find ourselves shocked and defensive when someone accuses us of acting on them. We are wholly unaware of our behavior, much less its underlying causes.

This is the difference between *objectivity* and *subjectivity*. Actors holding scripts are able to be objective because they can see the actions of their characters in the broader context of the play and the other characters in it. But in life, it's much more difficult to see the world beyond the prism of our own experience and self-interest. We see the world subjectively.

This applies not only to those who treat others unfairly as a result of their unconscious bias, but to those who are the targets of that treatment as well. It would take a kind of next level Zen mastery for Marie to leave this meeting and think, "Poor George and Steve. Their life experience has created in them an unconscious bias toward people of the opposite sex which does not allow them to see how their actions can have a negative impact upon the world. I shall pray for their enlightenment." It's more likely that she will leave deeply upset, feeling she has been demeaned, disrespected and robbed of her ideas.

So what can Marie do in this situation? What are her options? What actions could she take in this scenario to make the meeting go better for her?

Let's begin with her objective.

Marie enters the scene expecting it to be a standard business meeting and seems honestly blindsided when faced with George and Steve's disrespectful behavior. So while it might be tempting to think that Marie's objective is to overcome her co-workers' bias, that objective doesn't actually work here since she didn't know she would encounter that bias initially. I think Marie's objective is more straightforward: to inspire her colleagues to adopt her sales strategy through a dynamite presentation.

The obstacle she faces is the men's dismissive and disrespectful behavior toward her resulting from their unconscious bias.

So what tactics could she use to overcome that obstacle? (It's at this point in my presentation that someone will suggest a few extreme courses of action. Snatching the phones out of their hands and stomping on them is a popular one. Picking up a chair and hitting them with it is another.)

The first hint at the obstacle Marie will have to face happens before she even begins her presentation. In turning the meeting over to her, George introduces her as "pretty in pink Marie." Now George could argue, "What did I say? She's pretty and she's wearing pink. It's a compliment and a statement of fact!" But the remark is clearly inappropriate in the context of the meeting. George has addressed Marie in a way that makes her seem like less than the professional she really is.

In the scene, Marie just lets this moment go. But is that the right thing to do? Again, we have to take into account her relationship to George and their respective status. Marie would be perfectly in her rights to call George out on his remark, but it's not always that simple.

We also have to bear in mind the shock that Marie is probably feeling. Remember, she's not expecting to encounter this type of attitude. How many times in life have we been in situations where someone says something inappropriate to us and we find ourselves too taken aback to come up with a response in the moment? It happens to me all the time, and often it's not until hours later that I think to myself, "Oh, *here's* what I should have said! That would have been the *perfect* response!"

Assuming Marie were able to compose herself and respond thoughtfully in the moment, her best bet would probably be to try and bring the meeting back to a more professional level by asking George to refrain from making comments that are based on her appearance. This *might* serve to put George on notice that he has veered into murky territory and compel him to behave in a more professional manner. Maybe. Possibly.

Let's move on.

As Marie begins her presentation, the men immediately turn their focus away from her. They're on their phones, they're texting, they're doing anything other than giving her the attention and professional courtesy she deserves. What could she do here? This is where a lot of great suggestions have come up over the years from the women (and a decent number of the men) attending these programs.

One common suggestion is that she should ask questions. It's a great way to put George and Steve on the spot and ensure they're paying attention without being too confrontational. Another tactic is to stop speaking entirely -- an old teacher trick. Once they realize that Marie has stopped talking, it forces them to confront the fact that they weren't listening. Another approach is to ask them if she should continue her presentation at a better time, when they aren't so distracted. This one is a little more direct, but not so head on as to put anyone on the defensive.

What about the issue of having her idea stolen? If Marie's overarching goal is for George to adopt her sales strategy, then having Steve appropriate the idea and receive credit for it is a disaster for her.

Unfortunately for Marie, there's probably not much she can do in this situation. Sure, she could call them out directly and say, "Hey! That was *my* idea! Steve just stole it!" But given what we've seen of these two men, it's most likely that she would be met with the same blank stares I get when I suggest that this behavior -- hepeating -- is a common occurrence.

Instead, this part of the scenario often serves as a cautionary tale and a guide for what Marie can do in future meetings. The most common suggestion for Marie is that she should have her ideas written down (stamped? sealed? notarized?) prior to coming into the meeting. That way she can have something to point to that proves she was the one who came up with the idea, rather than having it become a she said/they said situation. It's unfortunate that this extra step should even be necessary and frankly unfair that the onus to solve the problem is put on her, but it's a reality that women often must face.

A Washington Post article from 2016 offered another good strategy -- albeit one that requires a little bit more planning -- called *amplification*. Female staffers in the Obama White House felt that men were appropriating their ideas in meetings, so they decided to come up with a way to make it stop. The strategy they devised was to agree that whenever one of the women put forth an idea, the other women in the meeting would immediately jump in and repeat the idea, peppering in the woman's name as often as possible. (*Great idea, Sarah. So what you're saying, Sarah, is that we should do 'X, Y and Z.' I really think that could work, Sarah. Thank you, Sarah, for suggesting that.*) This made it all but impossible for any of the men to repeat the idea later on and -- consciously or unconsciously -- pass it off as their own.

One reason that these tactics are so effective is that they address the issue of unconscious bias without pushing too hard against the boundaries of the workplace relationship. Another reason involves working styles and what we might call "comfort zones."

In her book *The Girl's Guide to Power and Success*, author and entrepreneur Susan Wilson Solovic notes that society has taught women from an early age not to be too bossy or assertive. One result of this is that men and women often have different priorities and approaches when working on a project. By and large, women tend to be more "process oriented," whereas men tend to be more "results oriented." So while women are focused on making sure that the process is fair, team members are getting along and everyone feels they have a chance to contribute, men are often focused purely on getting results with less consideration for how people may feel.

Another way Ms. Solovic suggests that social conditioning manifests itself is in what she refers to as the "but syndrome," where women will often begin a statement by offering a disclaimer along the lines of, "I don't know if this is going to work, *but* ..." or, "This might be a silly idea, *but* ..."

While this may be intended as mere politeness, it has the effect of diminishing both the message and the messenger. Ms. Solovic's advice? Drop the disclaimer and simply state the idea. It may feel a bit uncomfortable at first, but ultimately it makes the speaker appear more competent (and confident) and adds a sense of validity to the point they're trying to convey.

Now, having said all that, we know it's not just about comfort zones, don't we?

Gail Evans is a former executive at CNN who wrote a book called *Play Like a Man, Win Like a Woman*. In it, she points out that when a man is labeled as "aggressive" at work, the connotation is that he's bold and forceful, willing to do what it takes to achieve his goals. When a woman is labeled as "aggressive," it means she's viewed as hostile, mean and ruthless.

In short, a real b***h.

Most women I talk to know this. Most women I talk to have *experienced* this firsthand, and are understandably hesitant to act in a way that is too direct or aggressive, lest they be labeled as the office you-know-what.

Is this type of double standard right? I would argue no, as it's difficult to justify *any* type of double standard. But beyond being wrong on a moral level, it's not particularly smart on a financial level either.

Women face a host of issues in the workplace, the most serious of which being sexual harassment, which we'll explore in greater detail shortly. But there are many less sensational -- and less talked about -- issues that nearly all women must deal with on a daily basis that stem from a kind of casual misogyny resulting from unconscious bias. We've focused on two of them here (demeaning comments and "hepeating"), and we can add other terms to the list including "mansplaining" and "manterrupting." Ms. Evans details a whole list of double standards that women have to deal with: the men can cry. You can't. They can be fat. You can't. They can have sex. You can't. The list goes on.

And then there are the numbers. As of this writing, women earn $0.82 to the male dollar; only 1 in 5 "C-Suite" leaders is a woman; women make up only 6.4% of CEO's in the Fortune 500. This in spite of the fact that women represent 47% of the workplace and have been earning more college and graduate degrees than their male counterparts for 30 years and counting.

All of which begs an obvious but perplexingly overlooked question: is a company going to be more or less profitable if *half* of its workforce feels undervalued?

It's incredibly challenging to try and see the world from someone else's point of view. I honestly believe that the shock, confusion and sometimes defensiveness that men so often express when they hear about unequal treatment of women in the workforce comes from a genuine place. *"I've been in the workforce for thirty years and this kind of thing has never happened to me. How can it possibly have been happening to all these other people without my knowing about it?"*

But reports of unfair treatment toward women are not isolated incidents, nor have they happened to only a few select people. And the numbers that reinforce the stories don't lie. Our little scene at the start of this chapter -- heightened for dramatic effect though it may be -- is not made up out of whole cloth. It's taken from the accounts of women all around the country from a wide range of industries. It's real, it's happening and it exacts a toll on both a personal and professional level.

As I said in the chapter on "Character," the point of this book is not to offer up a list of dos and don'ts. It's not an excuse to tell others how to behave or limit what they can or can't say. Ultimately, I believe people should decide how they act based on the best information they can obtain (with the understanding that our choices can and will have consequences). But that information is limited when we only consider our own point of view, and looking at the world the way an artist does -- with a greater sense of objectivity -- can give us a fuller picture.

As a man, I can never really know what it is to be a woman in the workplace. But I can listen to their stories and try to imagine how I might feel and act if faced with similar obstacles. It's not exactly the same as walking a mile in their shoes, but it's a step toward greater knowledge, better understanding and -- hopefully -- more compassionate behavior.

Scenes 4, 5 & 6

"A Simple Compliment"
"Asking for a Date"
&
"Turning the Tables"

At the time time of this writing, the issue of sexual harassment has exploded onto the national dialogue. High profile cases involving well-known figures in entertainment, sports and politics have dominated headlines and led to anti-harassment movements such as #metoo and #timesup.

These next few scenes will look at different aspects of this issue.

In the first scene, *A Simple Compliment*, Marie is seated at her desk. George, her boss, enters.

GEORGE. Hey, Marie. You got those papers for me?

MARIE. Sure. Right here.

(*MARIE hands GEORGE some papers.*)

GEORGE. Thanks. Is that a new outfit?

MARIE. Yeah. I just got it.

GEORGE. Hm. Looks good. I really like it.

MARIE. Thanks.

(*GEORGE exits.*)

***

So, what did George do in this scene? Was he acting inappropriately?

That all depends on how you interpret it. The only stage direction was Marie handing George some papers and George exiting, neither of which provides us any clues. Let's fill in that stage direction a bit and see where it takes us.

(*MARIE is seated at her desk. GEORGE enters.*)

GEORGE. Hey, Marie. You got those papers for me?

MARIE. Sure. Right here.

(*MARIE hands GEORGE some papers.*)

GEORGE. Thanks. (*Distractedly, half looking at the papers.*) Is that a new outfit?

(*MARIE stands to show off her new purchase.*)

MARIE. Yeah. I just got it.

GEORGE (*good naturedly*). Hm. Looks good. I really like it.

MARIE (*smiling*). Thanks.

(*GEORGE exits.*)

***

Now what do we think? It seems pretty clear that Marie and George have a cordial and friendly working relationship. George notices that the outfit is new, Marie is happy to show it off, George pays Marie a compliment and that compliment is well-received. All in all, it's about as pleasant and wholesome an office interaction as you're likely to see.

But what if we change those stage directions just a little bit ...

(*MARIE is seated at her desk. GEORGE enters.*)

GEORGE. Hey, Marie. You got those papers for me?

MARIE. Sure. Right here.

(*MARIE hands GEORGE some papers.*)

GEORGE. Thanks.

(*GEORGE looks up from the papers and notices MARIE's outfit. He steps closer and leers at her.*)

GEORGE. Is that a new outfit?

(*MARIE notices his stare and tries to cover herself up.*)

MARIE. Yeah. I just got it.

GEORGE. Hm.

(*GEORGE puts his hand on the back of MARIE's chair and leans within an inch of her.*)

GEORGE (*suggestively*). Looks good. I *really* like it.

MARIE (*uncomfortably*). Thanks.

(*GEORGE exits slowly, looking MARIE up and down as he makes his way out.*)

***

Was that interaction okay? Clearly not. Even though the words were exactly the same, the scene was entirely different.

In some of our other scenes, we've explored instances where a character's objective is perfectly benign, but their tactics are, at best, poorly chosen. In these two versions of *A Simple Compliment*, we actually see two very different objectives at play.

In version one, George enters the scene wholly fixed on the business at hand -- retrieving some papers he's asked Marie to prepare. As she passes the papers to him, her outfit catches his eye and he offhandedly asks if it's new. There are a couple of ways you could interpret this as an actor. You could decide that this is a question George reflexively blurts out because his eyes have caught something that stands out (a *physical discovery*), or you could take the approach that George is actively looking for ways to boost morale and sees Marie's new outfit as an opportunity to do just that by paying her a compliment. Either choice is valid (and there are certainly others) and retains the affable nature of the scene.

In version two, the objective is clearly more self-serving. Marie's outfit has caught George's eye in a way that awakens something primal, and he decides to act on that impulse.

Does George actually believe that leering and physical intimidation will woo her? Does anyone who acts this way believe such a thing? Most experts agree that this type of harassing behavior is not really about "wooing" or even sex, for that matter. It's about power. George wants to increase his own sense of power by taking Marie's power away from her.

This is a particularly tough one to play as an actor because the objective is so morally repugnant. When you see this desire to humiliate and dehumanize someone in all its naked ugliness, it's nearly impossible not to pass judgement. So how do you do it? For starters, we have to acknowledge that the desire for power is an instinct that's inside each of us to some degree. Ultimately we choose whether or not to *act* on this instinct -- and may look unfavorably on those who choose poorly -- but we can't deny that it's in us.

So as an actor, I have to put aside my personal feelings, focus on the overwhelming pull of this desire and imagine that, somewhere along the line, the character of George did not properly develop a sense of empathy.

This does not condone such behavior. This does not excuse it. This does not explain it away. But sexual harassment is a sad tale that is as old as time, and if we are to have any chance of fixing the problem, we have to start by understanding -- and honestly facing -- the root causes of it.

Let's take a look at one more version of this scene and then examine it more in-depth.

Asking for a Date

(*MARIE is seated at her desk. GEORGE enters.*)

GEORGE. Hey, Marie. You got those papers for me?

MARIE. Sure. Right here.

(*MARIE hands GEORGE some papers.*)

GEORGE. Thanks. You know, Marie ... now that you're working in my department, I was thinking it might be a good idea for you and I to get to know each other better.

MARIE (*uncertainly*). Oh?

GEORGE. Yeah. So I thought maybe, after work today, you and I could get together for a drink.

MARIE. Oh. Well, George, I'm just so swamped with work. I'm gonna stay here and work late tonight.

GEORGE. Oh. Okay. (*Pause.*) How about Friday night? We'll have dinner!

MARIE. Uhh ... my sister's coming in Friday night with her husband and their kids. I promised to babysit so they could go out and have a nice, romantic evening together.

GEORGE. Ah. I see ... Saturday night? Take in a movie?

MARIE (*at her wit's end*). Oooh. Um ... I forgot. They're staying with me the whole weekend. Actually, they might stay the whole *month*.

GEORGE (*exasperated*). Well what do I have to do to get you to go out with me?

***

Let's pause here and determine what George wants in this scene. We *could* infer a sexual motive, and we might even assume that this gets back to the desire for power that we explored in *A Simple Compliment*. But maybe we can put cynicism aside for a moment and assume that George's motives are more benign. Let's say that George wants to persuade Marie to go on a date with him. That seems clear enough.

The obstacle is equally clear -- Marie quite obviously does not want to go on a date with George. *Her* objective is to turn down his advances, but in this task she faces multiple obstacles. The first obstacle gets back to her relationship to George and our old friend status. Marie wants to turn George down, but she feels she must do so in such a way that won't upset him or make for an awkward working situation -- and possibly jeopardize her career. On a more compassionate level, Marie may simply be the type of person that hates to upset *anybody*, regardless of her relationship to them. So her tactic here is to try to get out of agreeing to a date by coming up with a series of excuses for why the particular times George is suggesting don't work. Her attempts at rebuffing his requests range from subtle to what we might term "subtle-adjacent."

George, however, seems either unable or unwilling to take no for an answer. Why is this?

If he's unable, it could be that he's just not the type of person that *gets* subtlety. If he's unwilling (which I think is the more likely answer), this could be another instance where societal conditioning has created a blind spot for George. There's this myth that's been perpetuated that when a woman rejects a man's romantic advances, she's either being coy or just needs to be *convinced* that he's right for her.

It's the oldest story in the Hollywood playbook. A young man meets a beautiful, interesting woman and is instantly smitten. He must have her! But alas, she's engaged to someone else. Or she finds him too crass. Or she's about to become a nun. Or a million other variations of this old trope.

But it's no use. Our hero is determined. She's got her claws in him and he will not rest until she is his! He persists and persists and persists until one day, one *moment*, she realizes that *love was standing in front of her the whole time!!*

Did I forget to say spoiler alert? I forgot to say spoiler alert. Sorry. Hope I didn't ruin the movie for you.

Whatever the reasons -- George's ignorance or arrogance -- Marie's attempts at subtlety have not helped her achieve her objective. Perhaps the best thing for her to do is just be straightforward and tell George that she does not want to go out with him. Let's pick the scene back up and give that a try.

What could possibly go wrong?

GEORGE (*exasperated*). Well what do I have to do to get you to go out with me?

MARIE. Actually, George, I just don't feel comfortable going out with you, with us working together and you being my boss and all. I'm afraid I'm gonna have to say no.

GEORGE. Oh. Okay. Hey, no big deal. I just thought it would be good for us to get to know each other.

(*GEORGE turns and begins to exit.*)

GEORGE (*to himself, but loud enough that she can hear*). Because bonuses *are* coming up ...

***

And now we're right back to the abuse of power.

You may have noticed that George never actually says, "Go out with me or you won't get your bonus." Likewise, he never says anything in *A Simple Compliment* beyond "nice outfit, I really like it." But the threat here is implied, setting up a *quid pro quo* scenario. Without overtly stating it, George is letting Marie know that if she says yes, she'll get her bonus. If she says no, Christmas is going on the credit card.

What's been depicted in these scenes are examples of the two forms of sexual harassment recognized by law -- hostile work environment and *quid pro quo*. And to be honest, these depictions are fairly mild compared to the many stories we are hearing at this moment.

As I mentioned at the start of the chapter, the issue of sexual harassment currently is dominating the news cycle, and rightfully so. But anyone who's been paying attention knows that, while the *reporting* of this problem is new, the problem itself is not.

In 2016, the Equal Employment Opportunity Commission released a report on the state of sexual harassment in the workplace. This report was the result of an 18-month investigation by a special task force whose goal was to determine how much progress had been made in curbing sexual harassment in the thirty years since the Supreme Court ruled that it was a violation of Title VII of the 1964 Civil Rights Act. Their conclusion -- which we're seeing illustrated in these media reports -- was that, while *some* progress has been made, sexual harassment remains a problem that is both serious and pervasive.

The EEOC handles roughly 90,000 charges of workplace violations every year, and they state that fully one-third of those cases involve some aspect of harassment. The year of the EEOC's report, around 8,000 cases dealt explicitly with sexual harassment.

When you consider the vastness of the American workforce, 8,000 incidents of sexual harassment may not seem like that big a number. But the EEOC is quick to point out -- and this is backed up by the National Women's Law Center -- that the number of incidents *reported* is only a fraction of the number of incidents that actually take place. What the report found is that when someone is the victim of sexual harassment, the three actions that they're most likely to take are (1) avoid the harasser, (2) attempt to downplay the severity of the harassment in their own mind or (3) make a conscious effort to forget that the harassment ever took place.

The action that a victim of sexual harassment was *least* likely to take? Report it.

That's a striking enough statement that I think it bears repeating. The action that a victim of sexual harassment is least likely to take is to report it, either internally or to an external agency such as the EEOC or the National Labor Relations Board.

Often this hesitance to report harassment is due to a fear of retaliation. Sometimes it's the fear that a kind of stigma or "victim blaming" will be attached. Often it's the fear that they won't be believed (as we saw in the recent case of Dr. Larry Nassar, where years of abuse allegations made by dozens of female Olympians fell on deaf ears). And sometimes it's just out of a sense that nothing is going to be done about it. The victim comes to believe that this is how it is, how it always was and how it ever shall be.

With so few incidents reported, it's impossible to know how many women are victimized by sexual harassment in the workplace every year. And while the human cost is the most important aspect, companies have to consider the financial costs as well.

The year that the report came out, the EEOC collected $164.5 million in damages on behalf of victims of sexual harassment. But that's just damages paid. That figure doesn't take into account associated legal fees, nor does it consider the multitude of other ways that sexual harassment can affect the bottom line such as lost productivity and brain drain through organizational turnover as victims seek employment elsewhere. It also fails to account for the damage to a company's reputation if word of the harassment leaks out (shareholders jump ship, consumers boycott products, etc.).

I have yet to see a comprehensive analysis of the cost of sexual harassment in this country per year (I've seen a few different studies, and the results tend to vary). But someday soon, someone is going to put that study together. And when they do, the numbers are likely to be astronomical.

***

Let's take a look at one last variation of this scene.

Turning the Tables

(*GEORGE is seated at his desk. MARIE, his boss, enters.*)

MARIE. Hey, George. You got those papers for me?

GEORGE. Sure. Right here.

(*GEORGE hands MARIE some papers.*)

MARIE. Thanks. (*Pause. MARIE sets the papers back on the desk.*) You know, George. I was thinking ... you and I should get together some time.

GEORGE (*surprised*). You and me?

MARIE. Sure. (*She leans into him, exposing some cleavage.*) Go out. Have dinner. See a movie.

GEORGE. Uhh ... I just got divorced. I don't have any money left!

MARIE. Ooh, that's all right. (*She puts a hand on his shoulder and leans even closer.*) I'll come over to your place. I'll make dinner. Maybe bring over some wine ...

GEORGE. Actually, I've got the kids all weekend.

(*MARIE sits in GEORGE's lap.*)

MARIE. All the more reason we should get together. So you can ... *relax* before the weekend.

GEORGE. I don't know ...

(*She rubs her fingers through his hair.*)

MARIE. Think about it, George. Dinner. Wine. A movie ... *me*.

***

Let's pause the action before things get too hot and heavy.

So what does Marie want in this scene? In the interest of discretion, let's just say she wants George.

In performance, this scene is usually good for some big laughs, particularly when you have two actors capable of capturing the awkwardness of the moment. But the point is fairly obvious. While sexual harassment is heavily skewed toward women, it's not gender specific. Harassment is harassment is harassment.

***

The roots of sexual harassment run deep, with motivations sometimes so psychologically buried that the perpetrators are unable to see it in themselves even when it's pointed out to them. And that's exactly why the issue needs to be brought out into the open and talked about. It often takes time and repetition to realize the cause of an issue and to start taking steps to deal with it. Rooting out inappropriate behavior isn't always about finding fault in others. Sometimes it's about acknowledging the fault in ourselves.

Every day, more accusations of sexual harassment come to light. At a time such as this, it can seem inappropriate, if not outright tasteless, to talk about "silver linings," particularly for the victims, many of whom may spend years trying to overcome the emotional and psychological damage caused by the abuse they've endured. But we can, at the very least, take advantage of the fact that this subject is now top of mind for so many people. A discussion has begun, and a movement has begun with it. It doesn't heal the victims and it doesn't solve the problem overnight. But it's a start.

Scene 7

"Happy Hour"

The past several scenes looked at sexual harassment in the workplace. But what about *outside* of the workplace? Do the same rules still apply?

In the scene that follows, George once again approaches Marie at her desk. This time, they are colleagues of equal rank.

(*MARIE is seated at her desk. GEORGE enters.*)

GEORGE (*cheerfully*). Good morning!

MARIE. (*sullen*). Good morning.

GEORGE. How are you coming with those copy revisions?

MARIE. You'll get them when I'm done.

GEORGE. Is there a problem?

MARIE. *You're* the problem.

GEORGE. Me?

MARIE. You're disgusting.

GEORGE. Because I asked you about copy revisions?

MARIE. You're such a jerk.

GEORGE. What are you talking about?

MARIE. I'm talking about last night.

GEORGE. Last night? You mean at happy hour?

MARIE. Who the hell do you think you are?

GEORGE. Look, we were all just having a good time.

MARIE. I was having a good time too, until you started with that "forbidden dance" stuff.

GEORGE. Pretty cool, huh?

> (*GEORGE shows off some of his "forbidden dance" moves.*)

MARIE. I don't call drooling all over me at the bar and whispering those filthy things in my ear "cool."

GEORGE. Hey, it was happy hour. I was being *happy*.

MARIE. Well, you made me *un*happy. We may have to work together, but I don't have to put up with that kind of abuse.

GEORGE. Whoa, whoa, whoa. Hold on a minute. We weren't at the office. We were in a bar. It was *happy hour!*

MARIE. Well go be *happy* somewhere else. I've got work to do.

GEORGE. But I wanted to talk to you about the new project.

MARIE. I'm busy. Send me an email.

GEORGE. Oh. Okay. (*pause*) So ... see you at happy hour tonight?

(*MARIE faceplants on her desk.*)

***

It's getting harder and harder to advocate for George. We'll put him in a better light in another chapter, but for now let's try to look at this scene as dispassionately as possible.

George enters completely oblivious to the fact that he has upset Marie. As far as he knows, they're two co-workers who get along great both inside the office and outside. Marie, however, is fuming. George crossed the line last night at happy hour, and Marie has been stewing about it ever since.

Marie is quick to call George out on his behavior (as well she should), but George doesn't get it. From his perspective, they were just enjoying a few drinks after work and "having a good time." If things get out of hand, what's the big deal?

Looking at this example, it seems pretty clear that George and Marie's working relationship has been damaged by George's behavior at happy hour. That should be enough to say that the principles of respect in the workplace do indeed apply outside. But from a legal perspective, the issue isn't that black and white.

While rules prohibiting harassment *in* the workplace are pretty clear cut, there is in fact no law that defines an employer's right to fire an employee for incidents that occur *outside* of the workplace. This essentially leaves companies to come up with policies regarding conduct outside of workplace on their own, without any clear legal guidelines. Most companies do indeed have such rules in place, but they have less motivation to enforce those rules knowing that they're unlikely to face a lawsuit if someone misbehaves when they're off the clock.

But what you can be fired for -- and what a company can be sued over -- shouldn't be the only guiding force for how we behave. Laws and company policies certainly help to curtail some types of behavior, but decency and common sense have their place as well.

George and Marie's ability to work together has been compromised by the events at happy hour. While there may be no immediate repercussions, the potential for long-term damage is high. Not following the same rules of respect toward a colleague outside of the workplace may not get you fired, but it certainly fails the test of being either the right thing to do or the smart thing to do.

Scene 8

"People Will Talk"

Now that we've looked at behavior outside of the workplace, let's dig a little deeper into how that behavior might creep into the workday.

George, Steve, Carol and Marie are scheduled for an early morning meeting to discuss strategies for a new project. Marie is running a little behind, and George and Carol think they might know why ...

STEVE. Are we early or is Marie late?

GEORGE. Oh, *we're* on time.

CAROL. I wouldn't be surprised if she didn't make it in at all.

GEORGE. Not after last night.

(*GEORGE and CAROL share a laugh.*)

STEVE. What happened last night?

CAROL. You didn't hear?

STEVE. Hear what?

GEORGE. Seems like our friend Marie really know how to par-tay.

STEVE. Marie? I always thought of her as the serious type.

CAROL. Nu-uh ...

GEORGE. The truth's out now.

CAROL. She is *so* busted.

STEVE. What are you two talking about?

GEORGE. Last night, at the bar down the street? Marie was out of control.

CAROL. Totally.

STEVE. Really? What'd she do?

CAROL. Well, let's just say that the last time I saw Marie, she was drinking way too much, talking way too loud and getting all sloppy with that good looking guy from accounting.

GEORGE. What's his name? Randy?

CAROL. I think *she's* the one who was "randy."

GEORGE. I heard she was undressing him at the bar.

CAROL. I heard she was undressing *both* of them at the bar.

STEVE. Wait, you guys saw Marie taking her clothes off?

GEORGE. I didn't actually *see* it. Heard about it from some other guys who were there.

CAROL. Me too. They said she was really wild.

STEVE. Hold on. Did you actually *see* her doing anything?

GEORGE. Well, I had to leave early to get home. But the other guys said that after I left she started going crazy.

CAROL. Oh, yeah. Everyone's talking about it this morning. Our Marie is front page news.

STEVE. But neither of you *actually saw* --

(*MARIE enters.*)

MARIE. Morning, guys! Sorry I'm late. Traffic, right?

(*GEORGE, CAROL and STEVE stop talking and avoid making eye contact with MARIE.*)

MARIE. I thought up a great new approach to the project. I can't wait to tell you my idea. It's brilliant. You're gonna love it!

> (*GEORGE and CAROL break into spontaneous laughter as STEVE pulls out his phone and tries not to engage.*)

MARIE. What? What?

***

What do we think happened last night? Was Marie out of control? Did she cross the line?

The point, of course, is that we don't know. What we have here is idle gossip and secondhand reports. But is it really "idle" gossip? Is it harmless? And if Marie was indeed out of control at the bar last night, is *that* an issue which needs to be addressed?

Let's look at the situation from each character's point of view. George and Carol were out with Marie the previous evening. Marie had a few drinks and began flirting with a coworker. That much George and Carol can agree on. Beyond that point, it all becomes conjecture. Other people who were there *claim* to have seen Marie go "crazy," but George and Carol can't actually vouch for that.

So if no one knows what really happened last night, why would you take up valuable work time talking about it?

Let's be honest here -- because it's *fun*! If I thought that a coworker was going wild at some bar, I'd talk about it too! Most people would, and there are some solid arguments to be made for why a certain amount of gossip in the workplace can be a good thing. Let's return to that in a moment.

Steve really comes off as the voice of reason here. He quickly notices some red flags in the account of last night's scene at the bar and tries to clear them up. Over and again he presses George and Carol on whether or not they actually saw -- with their own eyes -- any of the things Marie is accused of doing. But George and Carol aren't having it. They saw enough in the early part of the evening to make the stories they've heard about Marie seem plausible, and they're having too good of a time sharing these juicy bits of gossip to listen to Steve being all *practical*.

Then we have poor Marie entering the scene with no idea that she's been the talk of the morning. She bursts in, excited to tell her colleagues about a great idea she's come up with, only to find herself being laughed at for reasons she doesn't understand. Anyone who's ever suspected they're being ridiculed behind their back knows what a sickening feeling that is.

The issue here isn't whether Marie got a little out of control the night before, but where the line exists *in the workplace* as far as gossiping goes.

As I mentioned, there's an argument to be made that a certain amount of gossip can be a good thing. It can strengthen camaraderie (at least among those who aren't the *subject* of said gossip), serve as a welcome distraction from a stressful workday and allow us an opportunity for some much needed venting.

A study by Stanford University goes even further, saying not only that gossip can have positive effects, but that eliminating gossip in the workplace altogether can actually do serious damage. Gossip allows us to hold people accountable, calling out behaviors that can be harmful or negative to a larger group or even the company as a whole. The study found that when people who behaved selfishly were ostracized by other members of their peer group, they often picked up on that negative vibe and began working more in a spirit of collaboration. In other words, gossip can serve as a check on selfish behavior and incentivize people to come back to the fold.

But gossip can also cross the line, tarnishing the reputations of those who don't deserve it and creating a toxic work environment. And if you're having trouble figuring out where that line exists, you're in good company. It's an issue that courts are still wrestling with as well.

In 2013, a woman who worked at a private technical school in Atlanta filed a complaint with the EEOC against one of her managers alleging sexual harassment. Shortly thereafter the woman was fired, not for filing the complaint (which would have been a clear case of retaliation), but because she discussed the issue with a colleague, and the school said that this discussion violated their "no-gossip" policy. The issue was eventually taken up by the National Labor Relations Board, and the judge in the case ultimately struck down the school's no-gossip policy, declaring it "overly broad." Specifically, the judge stated that the policy violated Section 7 of the National Labor Relations Act which classifies any discussion of wages, hours and other employment conditions as protected speech.

What's striking to me is that the school would have been well aware of Section 7 of the NLRA when drafting their no-gossip policy, but still felt comfortable making it as broad as they did and using it as justification for firing this employee. The reason for that lies, I think, in a certain vagueness in the NRLA's language, particularly the phrase "other employment conditions." It's a phrase that leaves a lot open to interpretation, and whenever you have ambiguity, you're going to have lawsuits.

We've looked at some of the benefits of gossip in the workplace, but in order to figure out when it crosses the line, we need to identify some of the dangers.

For starters, there is the erosion of trust and morale, as well as increased levels of anxiety as rumors begin to circulate regardless of facts. Think of poor Marie walking into that scene and finding herself the laughing stock of a joke she's unaware is even being told. How is she supposed to carry on with the rest of the day as that sense of fear and paranoia continues to fester? How would *you* manage that anxiety?

Other dangers of gossip include divisiveness in the workplace as employees take sides, which in turn is going to lead to lower morale and lost productivity. There is also the damage that can come to someone's reputation, and the possibility of attrition as good employees leave what they view as a toxic work environment.

Here's another aspect of this situation to consider. What if Marie really has a problem? What if this isn't an isolated incident, but part of a larger pattern of alcohol abuse? What if her drinking is affecting her work, or her relationship with her co-workers?

If that's the case, then gossip probably isn't the way to handle it. George and Carol wouldn't be doing Marie a favor by joking about her behavior behind her back. If they were genuinely concerned for her as a friend, they would want to speak with her directly and let her know that they think she may have a real problem. And if the concern were more about how it was affecting her work (and, ultimately, the work of the team), then that's the time to have a conversation with either her boss or HR.

So where do we draw the line on gossip? At the end of the day, this may be a situation where the best policy is to rely on the old golden rule. If you're saying the kinds of things you wouldn't want said about you, maybe it's just better to hold your tongue.

Then go home and gossip with your spouse about it.

Scene 9

"Under Pressure"

Our last scene explored the dangers of talking about someone behind their back. But face to face communication has its hazards as well. In this scene, Carol is a claims specialist under a lot of pressure. Marie is a recently hired assistant.

CAROL (*agitated*). Marie, can you come in here please?

MARIE. Sure, Carol. Just let me finish--

CAROL. *Now*, Marie.

MARIE. Coming.

(*MARIE hurries into CAROL's office.*)

CAROL. Marie, I want to ask you something. Do you have a problem with your hearing?

MARIE. My hearing? No, I don't think so.

CAROL. Because if you have a problem with your hearing, we can arrange for you to visit an ear doctor.

MARIE. No, I'm pretty sure my hearing's okay.

CAROL. Then why is it that yesterday, when I asked you to release payment on the Taylor account, you didn't do it?

MARIE. You never asked me to release payment on that account.

CAROL. Of course I asked you. I even left you a note. Maybe it's not your ears. Maybe it's your eyes. Maybe what you *really* need is an eye doctor.

MARIE. You never said anything and you never left me a note to release that payment.

CAROL (*waving a finger in MARIE's face*). Oh, no. Don't you even *try* that with me.

MARIE. Carol, I don't understand.

CAROL. And I don't understand how someone can be so incredibly incompetent at their job!

MARIE. I'm good at my job.

CAROL. Good at it?! You can't even follow the most simple, basic instructions!

MARIE. Please, Carol.

CAROL. Excuse me. I'm speaking at the moment. Do not interrupt me.

MARIE (*sheepishly*). Sorry.

CAROL. Thank you. They're breathing down my neck to make the target numbers. I cannot afford to have my work messed up by some sloppy, lazy, stupid person who doesn't know how to do her job.

MARIE. Carol, I don't think you should speak to me like that.

CAROL (*mocking her voice*). *I don't think you should speak to me like that.* Well let's just see if I can arrange it so that no one at this office ever has to speak to you again.

MARIE. Please, Carol, I need this job. We're just getting caught up on bills and--

CAROL (*dismissively*). Just go. I have work to do.

MARIE. If there's anything I can do--

CAROL. *Just. Go.*

(*MARIE exits visibly shaken.*)

CAROL (*to herself*). Why is it so hard to find good employees?

***

So ... what do we think of Carol's management style?

I should point out here that if there's one scene in my presentation that's an outright commercial for HR, it's this one. Carol's behavior is clearly unacceptable for a manager (or anyone, for that matter). She bullies, intimidates and harasses Marie throughout the scene, attacking everything from her intelligence to her looks, questioning her competence and threatening her job. She even resorts to the old playground tactic of mocking Marie when she attempts to stand up for herself. Carol comes off as a monster, and in the hands of a talented actress who can really dig into the nuance of the moment, that effect is magnified.

And yet ...

After getting my audience riled up by asking them to point out some the specific things Carol did or said that they found inappropriate, I ask if any of them has any sympathy for her. She is, after all (as the title of the scene would imply), under a lot of pressure.

In fourteen years of doing these presentations, I've never had anyone answer yes to that question. I'm guessing I'd be hard pressed to find anyone reading this book who would answer yes either.

So let me play devil's advocate.

This isn't little league. It's not elementary school. These aren't children. These are adults in the professional world, and mistakes can have dire consequences. So, with that in mind, can we justify Carol's behavior?

I imagine the answer is still no, as it typically is in my training program. But I also bet you had to think about it a little, didn't you?

Let's look at this scene from Carol's point of view. As she points out, she has people that she has to answer to herself, and those people are really pressuring her to perform. She knows she can't do everything on her own, so she needs the people working for her to be just as motivated as she is. Maybe this can work as Carol's objective: to motivate Marie to work at maximum capacity and efficiency.

Again, not a bad goal. Properly motivated employees not only help the company, but stand out on their own and have a better chance of rising up the corporate ladder. So once more we see that the underlying objective is a positive one. It's the tactics Carol employs that are the problem.

The angry boss calling an employee into their office and reading them the riot act is a scene we see played out over and over again in popular culture. It's practically a staple in the movies.

Back in 2005, a book detailing a "formula" for writing a Hollywood screenplay called *Save the Cat* was published, and it became such gospel in the film industry that its influence can be seen in nearly every major Hollywood picture made since then. A crucial part of that formula calls for the main character to be "dressed down" by a superior within the first 15 minutes of the film, thereby showing us the seriousness of the situation and overtly stating the movie's theme. (Seriously, watch any major studio film, in any genre, made since about '06 and you will find this scene.)

In sports, we see images of the gruff coach furiously bellowing away at his players in an attempt to inspire them to greatness. The same goes for reality weight loss shows, cooking shows and nearly every other type of competition. In fact, we see this scenario repeated so many times that it may become tempting to think that this really is the best way to get the most out of people. "Yes, I'm screaming at you! *But it's because I CARE!!*"

But does it work? The numbers would argue it does not.

When managers project their own stress onto their employees, they create a chronically stressful work environment. According to a study done by Eastern Kentucky University, 40% of workers in this country describe their jobs as very or extremely stressful, with 1 in 4 reporting that the stress is constant and unrelenting. It doesn't stop at the end of the workday. People are taking this stress home with them.

Why is this so bad? Because when a person is under stress, the brain responds by dumping a chemical into the body called cortisol. In short doses, this is a helpful and necessary component of the "fight or flight" response. But if cortisol continues to be produced consistently over a long period of time -- as it does when a person is experiencing chronic stress -- it can elevate blood sugar to dangerous levels and lead to a myriad of health problems including heart disease, obesity, diabetes, insomnia, depression and more.

With so many people undergoing chronic stress, it's estimated that stress related illness costs companies in the U.S. $300 billion every year. Yes, that's billion with a "b." (And it's not just in this country. The United Nations International Labor Organization has labeled occupational stress as a global *epidemic*.)

A report from Fairleigh Dickinson University supports these findings, but then goes on to note that *acute* stress is actually a very good thing. This is the kind of stress we experience when something goes unexpectedly wrong, or a deadline is fast approaching with a project only half finished. At these moments, everyone in the office must band together, marshal their energies and work on solving the problem as a team. This leads to a spike in energy and an increase in creativity and productivity.

But acute stress is momentary, which implies that the usual status quo is a relatively low stress environment. A problem comes up, there's a *moment* of high stress, the problem is dealt with, and the office returns to its state of relative calm. Chronic stress, on the other hand, lasts all the time, kills creativity and productivity, and ultimately costs companies hundreds of billions of dollars every year.

So what we see in this scene is that the tactics Carol uses actually work *against* her achieving her objective. The more stress she puts on poor Marie, the less likely she is to get good results. Marie will become more fearful, more inhibited and more likely to make mistakes as the stress piles up.

(I should point out here that the issue of whether Carol really did ask Marie to release the payment -- or leave a note for her to do so -- is immaterial. Regardless of who is right and who is wrong, Carol is doing a disservice to herself and to Marie by using tactics such as bullying, threatening and harassing.)

While we may not be able to muster much sympathy for Carol in this scene, we can, at least, understand what might lead her to behave as she does. In her book *The Fear Free Organization*, clinical psychologist Joan Kingsley examines the role that fear plays in the workplace. Rather unsurprisingly, she finds that the number one fear that employees have is the fear of losing their job. This applies not just to the rank and file who may feel that they're most at risk. The fear is reported across the whole employee spectrum, from entry level all the way to upper management.

In our scene, Carol is clearly under stress herself, and she is acting out of the gut instinct of fear and self-preservation. It's unlikely that she's a pure sadist who delights in torturing her subordinates. Rather she's succumbing to the same pressure being put on her from her own superiors.

So how can Carol break this cycle of stress (and ultimately achieve the results she's looking for)?

There's no shortage of books and articles that offer strategies for dealing with stress in the workplace, and while many of these publications may boast of offering the "secret" to stress management, some common themes and practices emerge. The most common strategies -- and these are backed up by the American Psychological Association -- involve developing healthy habits outside of work. Regular exercise, good eating habits and staying on a regimented sleep schedule have all been shown to reduce the effects of stress. Sharing your concerns with friends and family is also helpful, as is writing your feelings in a journal.

Ultimately, the strategies for coping with stress are pretty straightforward, but that doesn't mean they're easy to implement ... or stick with. Many of us try to cope with stress by doing the exact opposite of what would actually help us. We eat bad food, drink too much and push our feelings deep down where we don't have to face them. Much like Carol projecting her stress onto Marie, our attempts at reducing stress by indulging in negative behaviors work against us.

It's not easy to take the steps necessary to deal with the many stresses that come with our jobs. It's an act of will sometimes. But if we want the workplace to be an environment where we can be at our best -- and where we can get the best out of others -- then doing the hard thing is often what's required in order to achieve our objectives.

Scene 10

"Roommate"

Difficulties with face to face communication aren't exclusive to the manager subordinate relationship. In this scene, Carol and Marie are colleagues of equal rank. Marie is returning to work after missing a day with the flu. They meet in the break room.

MARIE. Hey, Carol. Thanks for covering me yesterday. That flu bug just wiped me out.

CAROL. Oh, no big deal. You know, I actually tried calling you at home when I couldn't get through on your cell. Um ... a *woman* answered the phone.

MARIE. Yeah. That was my roommate. I was at the doctor.

CAROL. I thought you lived with someone named Sean.

MARIE. I *do* live with someone named Shawn.

CAROL. Yeah, but I thought it was a *guy* named Sean.

MARIE. Well … Shawn is also a woman's name.

CAROL. Right, right, right. (*CAROL chuckles to herself.*) I never would've guessed.

MARIE. Guessed what?

CAROL. That you … *you know.*

MARIE. No, I don't know.

CAROL. Oh, come on. Why don't you just come … *out* with it?

MARIE. "Out" with it?

CAROL. Yeah. Like … *out of the closet* …

MARIE. Excuse me?

CAROL. Look, if you're gay, why don't you just say so?

MARIE. You, and this entire conversation, are *totally* out of line!

CAROL. Oh. Sorry.

(*MARIE exits.*)

CAROL (*calling after her*). So are you or aren't you?

***

Has Carol crossed the line? Seems fairly obvious that she has, but let's break it down.

What is Carol's goal here? We can speculate on any number of motivations, but let's start by identifying her immediate objective in the scene. In this particular moment, Carol wants to discover Marie's sexual orientation. Her obstacle is that Marie doesn't want to talk about this part of her life. Marie has made it clear that the topic is off-limits. Ultimately, Marie abruptly exits the scene and Carol is unable to achieve her goal (though Carol is plainly unwilling to let it go, calling out her question to Marie even after Marie has left the room).

Why does Carol want to know whether or not Marie is gay? What does she intend to do with this information? There are several viable explanations: she wants to get rid of Marie and is trying to dig up dirt; she has a crush on Marie and wants to know if Marie would be open to it; she's looking to form an LGBTQ support group and is on the hunt for more members. The list could go on.

Let's assume that Carol is trying to uncover sensitive information about Marie that could be used as leverage to force Marie out. Any reasonable person would have to conclude that Carol is in the wrong and should back off. But what if Carol's reason is more benign? What if she really likes Marie and wants to know if there's any chance of starting a romantic relationship? Or what if Carol just thinks of Marie as a close friend and is honestly curious about this part of Marie's life?

We could continue down this line of speculation but the answer will always come out the same -- it's not okay. Marie has drawn a line in the sand and that line should be respected. It's not a question of whether or not Carol's intentions are good-natured or dubious. Marie feels it's none of Carol's business. End of discussion.

Much has changed in attitudes regarding the LGBTQ community over the past generation as we've moved toward greater acceptance and inclusivity. When I was growing up in the 80s, homosexuality was something that was not accepted in most parts of society. Gays were openly referred to in derogatory ways, and those same slurs were regularly hurled around the playground by the young boys in my peer group. We may not have had any clue what those words meant, but the implication was that they were "bad."

The AIDS epidemic didn't help matters, at least not at first. There were many people who saw the crisis as proof that the "homosexual lifestyle" was wrong, with some going as far as to say that the disease was a punishment handed down from God.

But something else happened as a result of the AIDS crisis. Homosexuality came into the national conversation, as did the voices and faces of gay leaders. Those conversations shone a light on the humanity of that community, and they stopped being a people that lurked in the shadows of our consciousness. We began to see them for who they were -- our family members, our co-workers, our fellow human beings.

Soon after, media and entertainment began to change. Gay characters started appearing more often in movies and television, and while some of those portrayals may have been a bit stereotypical at first, as our attitudes have evolved, so have those characterizations.

Theater led the way in particular, with plays such as *The Normal Heart*, *Falsettos* and *Angels in America* opening our eyes and our consciousness to this previously curtained off world. Not only did we see more gay characters and LGBTQ-themed stories, but the artists who brought these works to life also began to make their sexual orientation known. Once upon a time, an actor coming out as gay would have been considered career suicide. Now the public barely bats an eye.

But despite all of the progress that's been made, discrimination still exists, and someone like Marie (assuming she identifies as other than heterosexual) may have sound career reasons to keep her private life private.

According to the Williams Institute, a UCLA Law think tank dedicated to research on gay rights in law and public policy, one in four LGBTQ employees report that they have experienced discrimination at the workplace in the last five years, and that same ratio of all LGBTQ adults -- a total of 2.2 million people -- say that limited job opportunities can make it a struggle just to put food on the table.

The numbers get even worse when it comes to transgender employees. The National Center for Transgender Equality reports that the unemployment rate for transgender adults is triple the national average, with over a quarter of that population reporting that they were either fired, not hired or denied promotion due to their gender identity.

One could get whiplash trying to follow the federal courts when it comes to protections for LGBTQ employees. Traditionally, Title VII protections from the 1964 Civil Rights Act have not extended to gay and transgender workers, but the tides there have been shifting. In the last two years of the Obama administration, the EEOC began using Title VII as a defense for LGBTQ employees in a couple of high-profile discrimination cases. They hadn't been directed to do this by the Department of Justice, but they weren't discouraged either.

In April of 2017, the 7th Circuit Court of Appeals upheld the use of Title VII as protection against discrimination on the basis of sexual orientation, and it looked like the tide had taken another major shift toward the advancement of gay rights. But just three months later, the Department of Justice under the Trump administration filed an amicus brief in federal court stating that it was *not* the position of the federal government to apply Title VII protections on the basis of sexual orientation or gender identity, and the tide shifted back.

Then in February of 2018, another federal court, the 2nd US Court of Appeals in Manhattan, defied the DOJ's missive by reaffirming the use of Title VII on the basis of sexual orientation, and just one month later, the 6th Circuit upheld the use of Title VII in a case involving gender identity.

Clearly this is an issue that is still, as the saying goes, "working its way through the courts."

There are a number of states (twenty, at the time of this writing) that offer protections against discrimination for employees on the basis of sexual orientation and gender identity, and two states that offer protections based on sexual orientation alone (but not gender identity). Most major companies do have non-discrimination policies that cover sexual orientation and gender identity or expression, but they are not bound to do so if they are in a state that doesn't require it. And without clear guidelines at the federal level, many companies may be less inclined to enforce existing policies.

If an employee chooses to keep their private life separate from their work life, that's certainly their prerogative, and co-workers would do well to respect those boundaries. But in situations involving sexual orientation and gender identity, the stakes can be much higher as there is still the potential for negative career repercussions. And if you've got an environment where people feel *forced* to conceal part of who they are, you're never going to get the best out of those employees.

In this instance, we don't know why Marie doesn't wish to discuss her private life, but we do know that we live in a society where people can face serious consequences if they reveal too much. And that's all the more reason to respect someone's choice to share or not to share the more intimate parts of who they are.

Scene 11

"Too Old"

People may find themselves excluded at work for a variety of reasons. We've just looked at how the LGBTQ community can face exclusion, now we'll focus on a few other groups who often struggle to be included.

In this scene, Steve is a veteran employee who has just inherited a much younger boss in Carol. The transition has been less than smooth, and Steve has asked Carol to meet with him to discuss the status -- and potential future -- of his role in the organization.

(CAROL enters STEVE's office.)

CAROL. What can I do for you, Steve?

STEVE. Carol, thanks for dropping by. This is a little difficult for me. Can I talk to you frankly?

CAROL *(impatiently)*. Sure, what's the problem?

STEVE. I just have this feeling that I'm not taken seriously around here these days.

CAROL. "Seriously?"

STEVE. It's just that recently I don't seem to be getting the best assignments.

CAROL. What do you mean?

STEVE. Well, for instance, the new project that came in last week? I see you put together a team to handle it and I couldn't help but notice that I wasn't included. *Again.*

CAROL. That's a very specialized project, Steve. It requires definite qualities for the team members.

STEVE. Qualities? What qualities, exactly?

CAROL. Look, this is a major account. We can't afford to blow this one. The people working on it are sharp and dynamic.

STEVE. You don't think I'm "sharp and dynamic?"

CAROL. They're high energy, hungry, cutting edge --

STEVE. What you're saying is they're young.

CAROL. I didn't say that.

STEVE. They're all in their twenties and thirties. The oldest one in the group is Karen Chang and I don't think she's thirty-five.

CAROL. Thirty-four, actually. Look, Steve, I really don't have to explain my decisions to you. But I will say that Karen has a lot of experience in this area.

STEVE. What about my experience? I've been in this field fourteen years, the last eight with this company. I've handled some of our most important accounts.

CAROL. Yes, I know. You contributed a lot in your day.

STEVE (*taken aback*). In my day? You make it sound like I've been put out to pasture. I still have a lot to contribute.

CAROL (*patronizingly*). Steve, you really shouldn't take this so personally. I don't know what you're so upset about. In a few years you'll retire. You can go fishing!

(*CAROL exits.*)

STEVE. I'm fifty. I'm not dead.

***

In any scene, as in any situation in life, there are small objectives and large objectives. In this scene, Steve has a larger objective of improving his position in the company, but *in the moment*, his focus is on the smaller (but no less important) goal of pressing Carol to admit that she has excluded him because of his age.

Is this a conscious decision on Carol's part, or another example of unconscious bias? This scene could go either way. Carol really might not see that she has been marginalizing Steve because he's older. On the other hand, it might be entirely intentional on her part. She might honestly view Steve as someone who is no longer relevant, and she's doing her best in this scene to assuage him with vague language and corporate speak, all the while keeping him on the bench. Either way, Steve's facing an uphill battle.

The fact is, it's in Carol's best interest to figure out a way to work with employees in Steve's age group. Right now in this country, the population is getting older. People are living longer and they're staying in their jobs long past traditional retirement age -- and for a variety of reasons. One of those reasons is necessity. According to the AARP, half of people age 50 or older have *less than $25,000* saved for retirement. The idea that they could quit the workforce and survive another twenty, thirty, possibly forty years on that amount of money is laughable.

But it's not only necessity. People are living longer in part because they're taking better care of themselves, and they often have no desire to cash in their chips just because they've hit some arbitrary date on the calendar.

I have a close friend whose mother is in her eighties. She's one of these people that's always on the go, bouncing from one activity to another. This has prompted an outcry from her friends and some members of her family who insist she must slow down. "Slow down, Sandy!" they cry. "You can't keep up this pace! You have to slow down!"

Her response is perfection. "I've seen people who slow down," she says. "It seems to me they just ... *slow down*."

I think that many people in my generation share this view. We've seen folks in the generation before us retire early only to wither and fade, whiling away the days watching reruns of *MASH* and *Murder, She Wrote*. And maybe that makes them perfectly happy. If so, good for them. Personally, it's not what I want for myself, and I think there are many who feel the same way.

Unfortunately, people staying in the workforce longer can create tension with younger employees. Some of that tension is due to simple differences in communication styles, and those differences are often intensified by technology. I heard an interesting story about just such a situation from an HR professional after one of my seminars. She told me about an over-fifty employee in her office who would never send a reply to emails. Instead, he would respond by picking up the phone and (gasp!) *calling the person who emailed him*. It would drive the younger people in the office crazy. "Why is he calling me?" they would wonder. "Just send me an email!"

Meanwhile, the older employee couldn't understand why everyone insisted on passing electronic notes all day when they could have an actual conversation instead. What seemed efficient to one side seemed a waste of time to the other.

These differences in communication styles can be frustrating, but they're typically counted as minor annoyances. The more serious tension between older and younger employees often comes from what economist Matthew Rutledge calls the "lump of labor fallacy." There's a belief among many younger people that employees staying on the job longer becomes an impediment to the younger generation being promoted up the ranks. It's understandable that this might be the perception, but it's hardly ever true. According to Mr. Rutledge, job performance is a much better indicator of whether or not one climbs the corporate ladder than age.

Economists also point out that staying in the workforce longer is good in a consumer based economy such as ours. The longer people stay employed, the longer they continue to spend.

It also means they spend less time collecting benefits from programs such as social security and medicare, which allows those programs to remain solvent.

And, of course, we have to look at what older workers bring to the workplace, which is, in a word, experience. Technology may change, but people, by and large, remain the same. Steve may not have grown up with smartphones and social media, but our *skill* in communicating with people is more important than what device we use to do it.

Along with that experience comes perspective. Things inevitably go wrong, and when they do, the outlook can seem bleak. But an employee who's been around awhile has seen just about everything and knows that most crises pass. While others are panicking, wondering if they'll be able to weather a particular storm, the Steves of the workplace can be a steady hand, able to guide others through rough waters.

Whether the Carols of the workplace like it or not, the Steves aren't going anywhere, at least not anytime soon. According to the Bureau of Labor Statistic, about 40% of people age 55 or older are still working, constituting 25% of the workforce. By marginalizing people in this age group, Carol robs herself of the opportunity to take advantage of this valuable human resource. Including them isn't a case of being nice to your elders. In today's workforce, it's a practical necessity.

Scene 12

"Wheelchair Bound"

Along with the increase in the overall age of the population comes an uptick in the number of Americans with disabilities. This scene will look at one scenario involving that demographic.

Marie is the head of a sales team. She's meeting with two of her top salespeople, Carol and George, to discuss a number of agenda items, including who should be assigned a new sales territory.

MARIE. The new territory looks *very* promising.

GEORGE. Time you assigned a sales rep.

CAROL. That's gonna be one lucky rep.

MARIE. You know who *should* get the assignment?

(*GEORGE and CAROL lean it, hoping it will be one of them.*)

MARIE. Ray.

(*Pause.*)

GEORGE. Ooh. Um ... do you really think he can handle it?

CAROL. Yeah. How's he gonna get into the buildings?

GEORGE. Will we have to arrange for someone to drive him to appointments? This could get to be a real pain in the neck.

MARIE. He has a car. He gets around. He's *earned* the job.

GEORGE. I wonder if the buildings in that neighborhood have ramps for his wheelchair. If they're even ... what do you call it?

CAROL. You mean "wheelchair accessible?"

GEORGE. Yeah, that's what I mean. You know, it seems like a lot to ask of *poor Ray*.

CAROL. I don't know if you'd be doing Ray a favor giving him this assignment.

GEORGE. *Should* you ask him?

CAROL. What if he couldn't handle it? You might just hurt his feelings.

GEORGE. You don't want to hurt his feelings.

CAROL. No, no, no.

GEORGE. Definitely not. Don't want to hurt his feelings.

(*Pause.*)

CAROL. You know ... this new territory's not all that far from *my* territory. I could take on some of it. Maybe even a *lot* of it.

GEORGE. I could pick up some of it, too. You know, now that I think about it, maybe a guy in a wheelchair isn't the right image we want to project for our company anyway.

CAROL. I can start calling for appointments on Monday.

GEORGE. Right. Monday.

MARIE. Okay, then. Let's move on to the next item on the agenda ... parking spaces.

***

"Poor" Ray. Good thing he has friends like Carol and George.
 Allow me to once again play devil's advocate. Is what Carol and George have done here really that bad? At the end of the day, these are salespeople, and it's in their best interest to go

after a promising new territory that could potentially earn them a higher commission. They've brought up concerns about Ray's ability to successfully perform his duties, Marie has listened to those concerns and she's made her decision accordingly. What's the problem?

Your answer likely depends on whether or not you subscribe to Machiavelli's idea that the ends justify the means. And in our society today, I would wager that most people don't. Indeed, to label someone as "Machiavellian" is to suggest that they are manipulative, calculating and dishonest.

Why we do something is at least as important as *how* we do something, and it's the how that's troubling here. Did Carol and George talk about Ray's performance history? His sales figures? Issues with customer satisfaction? No. What they did was played off of concerns about Ray's disability (much of it under the guise of concern for Ray's feelings). Carol and George have every right to make a case for why *they* should get the territory, but they don't have the right to smear a colleague in the process.

Marie bears a good degree of scrutiny here as well. It's not that she comes off as someone who hates Ray or hates people in wheelchairs. On the contrary, she opened by saying that Ray should get the territory. But she allowed George and Carol to manipulate her. She took their arguments at face value and lost focus of the fact that Ray's performance history had earned him the assignment.

You could say that Marie's heart is in the right place. As Carol and George paint the picture of a despondent Ray, crestfallen at his inability to maneuver around physical obstacles, Marie may feel genuine concern over Ray's emotional well-being. But in deciding to award the territory to George and Carol, she's robbed Ray of the opportunity to make that determination for himself. Difficult as the conversation may be, if Ray has earned the right to be considered for the assignment, then he should be allowed to decide for himself if he is up to the physical demands of the job.

And here I'll veer away from statistics and hypothetical scenarios and offer a story from my personal life.

My wife and I recently purchased our first home. (Living in the New York metro area, home ownership simply wasn't a reality for us. Moving to Knoxville, Tennessee, on the other hand, changed the financial picture considerably.) A few months after we moved in, my parents -- who live in Maryland -- asked if they could come visit for my son's seventh birthday.

I don't get to see my parents very often. Between my work schedule, my wife's work schedule and my son's school, summer camp and extracurricular activities, it can be difficult to get away. My parents are both retired, affording them much more flexibility, but in the past several years, my father's physical health has deteriorated rapidly. A combination of major back surgery, poor blood circulation in his legs and steadily advancing Parkinson's disease have severely limited his mobility. He's able to move around with the aid of a walker, but it's slow going. This makes travel difficult for them, and made getting into our New York apartment -- a fourth floor unit in a building with no elevator -- impossible.

So I was thrilled when they asked to visit and excited to welcome them into our new home. So excited, in fact, that it wasn't until a couple of days before their arrival that it dawned on me that there is no way to enter our house without climbing some stairs. The front door, the back door and even the entrance through the garage all have five or six steps.

As an able-bodied person, I simply didn't think about it. It's nothing for me to hop up those few steps and walk into the house. But for someone with a walker, it's much more challenging.

I wanted to find a solution on my own, so I looked into the possibility of renting a ramp. But to get a custom ramp required a company to come to our house, measure and assess the stairs and entrances and then deliver the right product. All of that took time that we didn't have. And even if we went that route, I was concerned that the ramp would be too steep. Images of my dad falling backwards and becoming seriously injured (or worse) filled my mind.

A day out from their trip, I started to panic. Fortunately, my wife -- who tends to be more level-headed about these things -- stepped in with a rational suggestion. Why didn't I just call my dad and explain the situation? He's the one with the walker, surely he should have the chance to weigh in.

But the truth was I didn't want to talk to him about it. It's difficult to watch your parents grow older and uncomfortable to discuss it with them openly. I was hoping that I could engineer a solution on my own and avoid an awkward conversation. Ultimately, however, my wife was right, and so I made the call. My dad's response? "Don't worry about it. We'll figure it out."

I wish I could say I heeded his advice, but not worrying wasn't on the table.

Finally the day arrived. They pulled up to the house and I met them in the driveway. Then my mom got out and together we surveyed the three entrances and tried to determine which one seemed the most accessible. Ultimately, we determined that the back entrance was best: it had only four steps that were fairly shallow and it was narrow enough that he could hold onto the guardrails on both sides.

The problem, however, was getting to those back steps. Several bushes and one tree pushed into the concrete walkway going from the driveway to the back door (a landscaping issue that we had put off addressing). My dad could walk back there, but it would require occasionally navigating his way off of the walkway and into the grass, something the walker was not well-equipped to do.

We talked it over with my dad and he agreed that this was best option, so we got him out of the car and began the journey. It took about ten minutes for him to get to the back of the house and up the steps, including short breaks to rest and plot out the best course. But eventually, through careful planning, steady pacing and sheer determination, he was able to make it into the house.

I eventually came to realize that it had been wrong of me to try and solve the problem for him. What I thought of as trying to spare his feelings was actually robbing him of the right to make his own decisions and to act on his own behalf. If I were in a similar situation (and it's likely that one day I will be), I would want that right for myself.

***

The picture that Carol and George paint of Ray as someone whose disability makes him unfit to be a successful employee is one that reflects an older attitude. You don't have to go back too far to see how much our society has evolved on this issue. Just watching old black and white movies, you hear some of the horrible terms used when talking about people with disabilities. They're referred to as "lame," "gimp," "cripple," "dummy," and the characters using these words aren't even trying to be mean. That's just the way people talked. The sense was that these people were "damaged" in some way and that it was okay to simply shunt them off to the margins.

Fortunately, the attitude today has become much more inclusive. But this doesn't mean that persons with disabilities are fairly represented in the workplace. According to the most recent census, 40 million Americans -- over 12% of the population --

report having a disability. That's a large demographic, and one that would be better served by including people with disabilities in the workforce. And yet the unemployment rate for the disabled is more than double the rate for non-disabled.

It can seem daunting to make accomodations for disabled employees, but the long-term benefits far outweigh any short-term difficulty. Grit and determination count for a lot in the workplace, and a person willing to go the extra mile to overcome a physical challenge can be a valuable asset. They may even serve as a source of inspiration to others. Ultimately, the limits of what a person with a disability can do are best determined by those who live with the challenge of overcoming that disability every day.

Scene 13

"Not Invited"

Let's take a look at one last scenario of exclusion. It's late on a Friday and most employees have left for the weekend. Carol, a recent hire, is working late, as are George and Marie.

(CAROL is seated in her cubicle. MARIE enters.)

MARIE. Hey, Carol. Don't work so hard. You'll make the rest of us look bad.

CAROL. Oh, hi, Marie. I'm just trying to catch up on a few things.

(MARIE smiles and crosses over to a file cabinet. GEORGE enters.)

GEORGE. Hey, Carol. How'd your first week on the job go?

CAROL. Hi, George. It went really--

GEORGE (*cutting her off*). That's great. (*Crossing to MARIE.*) Hey, Marie! You going to happy hour tonight?

MARIE. As soon as I sign off on a couple of forms. Just take a minute.

GEORGE. Tonight's Buffalo wings night!

MARIE. Yummy. But that's not the only thing on *my* menu tonight.

GEORGE. You mean the chicken fingers?

MARIE. I mean, I heard that there's about to be an opening for a director position in the Operations Department.

GEORGE. So?

MARIE. So, who never misses Buffalo wings Friday?

GEORGE. Ah-hah. Harry Thompson.

MARIE. The VP of Operations himself. I was thinking I might "accidentally" bump into him and *casually* let it slip that my experience would make me an incredible asset to his department.

GEORGE. That would mean a promotion, wouldn't it?

MARIE. It would indeed.

GEORGE. Hey! You hear anything about openings for me?

MARIE. Nope. But you never know what you can find out when people are relaxed and away from the office. (*Closes her folder and stands.*) Okay, let's go.

GEORGE (*looking over at CAROL*). Um ... you think we should invite Carol?

MARIE. Ooh. I don't know. You think she'd feel comfortable? Socializing with everyone? At happy hour?

GEORGE. She'd sure be out of place.

MARIE. I've never seen any of her crowd there.

GEORGE. I don't think she'd fit in.

MARIE. Yeah. Better to not put her in an uncomfortable position.

GEORGE. I think you're right.

(*CAROL crosses to GEORGE and MARIE.*)

CAROL. You guys have anything going on tonight? Or just going straight home?

(*MARIE and GEORGE exchange a panicked look.*)

MARIE. Uhhh ... No. Nothing on tonight.

GEORGE. Yeah. Just ... going straight home.

CAROL. Oh. Me too. Just going home.

(*Awkward pause.*)

CAROL. Okay. See you Monday.

GEORGE. You bet.

(*CAROL exits.*)

MARIE. Hey, we better hurry or they'll be all out of Buffalo wings!

GEORGE. I'm right behind you!

(*They exit.*)

***

What's going on in this scene? Why are George and Marie so hesitant to invite Carol to join them for happy hour?

The old saying goes that it's not what you know, it's who you know. Many people find this to be a fairly cynical statement, but there is a kernel of truth in there. Perhaps a better way to phrase it is that it's not who you know, it's who knows *you*. Having the right people know how talented, smart and dedicated you are may ultimately decide how far and how fast you rise in your profession. You may have the most beautiful singing voice in the world, but if you only belt out tunes in the shower, you're never going to make it on the big stage (depending, of course, on whose shower you're using -- but that's another story).

Marie and George know that a lot of the decisions made in the workplace are a result of things that happen *outside* of the workplace. Beer and Buffalo wings aren't the real reason they're attending happy hour. They have an agenda. They want to get some facetime with people who may be in a position to help them advance their careers in a setting that's less formal than the office. In this goal, Carol may be perceived as a threat. She's someone who is already exhibiting a strong work ethic and could challenge their bid to advance to a higher position.

This *could* be why they don't want to invite Carol to join them. But if you picked up on something else going on in the scene, you're not wrong. There's one crucial piece of information that's been left out -- in performance, Carol is always played by an African-American actress.

This is where the scene takes a darker turn. Carol is being excluded because of her race.

People can find almost any reason to exclude others. This scene would still work if Carol were muslim or overweight or in a wheelchair. It would work if Marie and Carol decided to leave George behind because he's a guy, or if it turned out that Marie really *was* gay (callback to scene 10) and Carol and George left *her* behind. But when it comes to race, that really does touch a nerve.

Here's a fascinating observation. In the discussion that follows this scene, I always ask the audience if they remember what Marie said when she and George were debating whether or not to invite Carol. Something about never seeing any of her ...

Nine times out of ten, someone in the audience will respond that Marie said she's never seen any of her "kind" there. The actual word Marie uses is "crowd," but this is such an obvious dog whistle that people almost always hear the word that was *intended* over the word that was said. In an odd way, I find this encouraging. People are so attuned to the hidden meaning behind that phrase that they actually hear the subtext.

None of this is to suggest that everyone *has* to hang out with everyone else outside of work. What people do in their free time is, of course, their business. But if there is an ethos of inclusion -- a sense that everyone is truly welcome regardless of their race, gender, religion, sexual orientation, etc. -- it can go a long way toward building a stronger, more harmonious and ultimately more profitable workplace.

Scene 14

"Monday Repeat"

A major component of my training programs is that they're "no-tech." I don't use PowerPoint, I don't show videos, I don't even use microphones. I want people to experience each event without any filters between audience and presenters. It's a way to not only shake things up a little, but to have the audience put away the screens for a while and connect on a human level.

But the fact is that technology is integral to doing business, and its application in the workplace means navigating a whole new way of communicating with one another -- which presents a unique set of challenges. These next couple of scenes will address some of those challenges in ways that might feel ... familiar.

In this first scene, George is head of operations at a chemical processing plant. He is about to begin the weekly team meeting.

GEORGE. Good afternoon, folks. I know we're all busy today, so let's just jump right into our weekly meeting.

CAROL. Sounds good, George.

GEORGE. First off, it appears there was an issue starting up the pumps this morning. Apparently, proper shutdown procedures weren't followed over the weekend and this led to a delay to start off the week.

MARIE. Wait. Didn't we cover this at *last* week's meeting?

GEORGE. Yes, I believe so, Marie. Carol, that's your team on the weekend shift. What's being done to address this problem?

CAROL. Well, George, I sent an email to Marie asking for her to clarify what issues her team was having with startup so that I could identify any problems with shutdown.

GEORGE. I see. Marie? Did you receive Carol's email?

MARIE. I did, George. And I immediately emailed you to request a copy of the updated shutdown procedures we received from corporate headquarters. Did you get that email?

GEORGE. I did, Marie. And I immediately emailed corporate and asked them to forward specific protocols with our newest models on to you. Did you get that email?

MARIE. No, I never heard from them.

CAROL. Oh, wait. *I* got that email. But I wasn't sure why corporate was emailing *me*, so I forwarded it to *you*, George.

GEORGE. Oh, that's right. I *did* get that email, Carol. But I thought I was just being cc'd, so I didn't look at it too closely.

CAROL. Oh.

MARIE. Huh.

GEORGE. Yeah.

(*Pause.*)

CAROL. So ... where does that leave us?

GEORGE. I'm not sure. Tell you what. Let's stick a pin in this one and we'll circle back to it at next week's meeting.

MARIE. Sounds good.

CAROL. Works for me.

GEORGE. Meeting adjourned!

(*GEORGE, CAROL and MARIE exit.*)

***

This scene usually produces an uncomfortable sting of recognition.
Rather than focus on all of the things that went wrong, let's try to put a positive spin on this and identity the things they did right. For starters, the fact that they're holding a face to face

meeting at all is a good thing. They've made sure to schedule time every week to meet in person so they can have a real discussion about the issues they're facing, as opposed to just sending out emails or relying on chance encounters in the halls..

Next, they've identified both the problem and the key people that need to be involved in order to solve it. They've also communicated the issue to the relevant players and gathered information that will be necessary as they work their way toward a solution.

It should also be noted that the overall tone of the meeting remained respectful throughout. An account was given of the steps that had been taken and who had been contacted along the way, but no one was thrown under the bus and no one felt they were being disrespected. The meeting was cordial and professional.

But as we can see, it's possible to maintain a respectful environment and still have a breakdown in communication.

Ultimately, the issue at hand is a lack of follow through. Business coaches talk a lot about follow through because the term lends itself so well to sports analogies. Swing a golf club or a baseball bat halfway and the ball isn't going very far. Throw a punch in the ring that stops just at your opponent's nose and you can be sure they'll still be standing at the end of the round. The analogies go on.

In our scene, the characters have done a good job of initiating action, but their efforts stall once they get tangled up in a web of who emailed what and to whom and how long ago and who was cc'd and who sent the attachment and --

It gets complicated.

This scene is actually part of a presentation we do on effective leadership, and in that context I would go on to suggest strategies for improving follow through. But I won't get into all of that now (I have to save something for the next book). I've included it here as an example of how technology throws another landmine into the already perilous field of human interactions. Understanding just how explosive that field can be -- and learning how to navigate it -- is an important aspect of maintaining a respectful workplace.

In this example, everybody involved is still able to get along. They haven't solved the problem, which is bad for the bottom line, but they're not at each other's throats either.

Unfortunately, not every miscommunication online is so pleasant ...

Scene 15

"Just Jokes"

George is seated at his desk. Carol, his boss, enters.

CAROL. George, can I speak to you for a moment?

GEORGE. Sure, boss. Always glad to talk to you.

CAROL. I need to ask you about something rather delicate.

GEORGE. Okay.

CAROL (*taking a printout from her folder*). Did you email these ethnic and sexual jokes to Karen?

GEORGE. Lemme see. (*He looks at the paper.*) Oh, yeah. I always send her jokes. See? There's my name. My jokes, my name.

CAROL. She's very offended.

GEORGE. You're kidding. When I tell these jokes at lunch she's always the one laughing the loudest.

CAROL. I asked her about that. She says she just laughs to fit in.

GEORGE. Really?

CAROL. She also objects that her name is on the distribution list. It makes her look like she *wants* to get these jokes. She says it makes her look unprofessional.

GEORGE. It does?

CAROL. She's filed a complaint with human resources.

GEORGE. She has? But I didn't mean any harm. They're just jokes!

CAROL. They're *very* inappropriate.

GEORGE. But everybody does it.

CAROL. We're not talking about everybody. We're talking about you.

***

Do you think that George is intentionally trying to offend anyone? That hardly seems the case. I would argue he's just trying to brighten a colleague's day by sending along some jokes that he believes she'll find funny, but he's gotten himself into all kinds of trouble.

It can be hard to know where to draw the line on humor in the workplace. Back in the early 90s, in the nascent days of email, the New York Times fired twenty-two people for email abuse after employees complained about receiving lewd jokes in their inboxes. Many of the people who lost their jobs claimed to have not even read the jokes themselves, saying they were simply forwarding material that had been forwarded to them. But the Times wanted to send the message that that type of joking -- whether in the breakroom, the cafeteria or over email -- was not to be tolerated.

Courts have ruled that companies have almost limitless rights not only to set email policies, but to monitor messages sent over personal computers, smartphones or other devices that are deemed company property. In 2010, one such case made it all the way to the Supreme Court.

Officer Jeff Quon, a member of the SWAT team in Ontario, California, was provided with a pager by his department and told that it was permissible for him to use the device to send personal messages provided he reimbursed the department for any overages. The arrangement was working just fine for everybody until the police department decided to conduct an audit of Quon's pager to determine how frequently he used it for personal rather than work related reasons. In the course of the audit, they discovered that Quon had been using the device to send sexually explicit messages to his wife ... *and* his mistress.

The department disciplined Quon, and Quon responded by suing the city of Ontario for violation of his 4th Amendment rights protecting him against unlawful search and seizure. The District Court ruled in favor of the city, but the 9th Circuit overturned that decision, ruling in favor of officer Quon. The case was eventually heard by the Supreme Court where the ruling was switched *again* in favor of the city of Ontario, with the court holding unanimously that the audit was work related and therefore did not violate the 4th Amendment.

While it's certain this won't be the last time the court is asked to weigh in on these matters, the decision in *Ontario v Quon* sets a precedent that companies will continue to be given a wide berth to monitor employee activity on company devices and software, and to take action if they feel any company policies have been violated.

***

Let's turn our attention back to the scene at hand. What if we put a little spin on it? What if Karen isn't offended by George's jokes at all? What if *nobody* in the office is offended? Does that make it okay? Does the company still have a right to tell George to stop?

This is where we begin to step into a broader culture war, with many people claiming that "political correctness" has run amok and nobody's allowed to say anything anymore. It's also where we run into some pretty gross misinterpretations of the 1st Amendment, as some confuse private consequences with being imprisoned by the state. (Put another way, you're not going to be sentenced by a court for telling a dirty joke. Court of public opinion, on the other hand, is another matter.)

You can liken this issue to having guests into your home. As the host, you have a right to ask your guests to refrain from telling any jokes that would be considered racist, sexist, etc., and you have the right to ask someone to leave if they don't respect your wishes. A company operates in much the same way. They have the right to set a certain tone for the office, as well as the right to impose consequences up to and including termination if employees can't abide by their policies.

We got a lot of pushback on this issue once during a presentation we did at a factory in Cleveland. Several employees told us that there was one table in the cafeteria that was known as the "trash table." This was where all of the racist, ethnic and sexual jokes were told, and if you didn't want to hear those kinds of jokes, you shouldn't sit there. And who the *expletive* were *we* to come in there and tell them what they could or couldn't say at *their* table?

What we finally had to point out was that it wasn't "their table." It was the company's table, and the company was just letting them sit there. I don't know if that message ever got through at the ground level, but management wanted to draw a line and they were well within their rights to implement restrictions on that kind of talk.

So where is the line on what material you can or can't send electronically? That's a line that might shift from company to company depending on where they want to draw it. But when it comes to using company technology, maybe a good rule of thumb is this -- if you wouldn't want your boss to read it, don't send it.

Scene 16

"Who Flies?"

What I've tried to do throughout this book is illustrate how each of us sees the world from our own point of view. Understanding that is the key to acting with greater respect toward our fellow workers (and, dare I suggest, our fellow human beings). "Before you judge a man, walk a mile in his shoes," goes the old saying.

In this final scene, we're going to walk that metaphorical mile in the shoes of Marie, George and Carol. One of them has to take a last minute business trip to California but no one wants to go. They've been asked to step into a meeting room and decide among themselves who flies.

MARIE. Okay, George. This one's got your name written all over it.

GEORGE. Y'know, normally I would go, but ...

CAROL. Yes?

GEORGE. My son has a big soccer game that week.

CAROL. *Soccer game?!*

MARIE. A "soccer game."

GEORGE. Yes. A soccer game.

CAROL. You never go to your son's soccer games.

GEORGE. That's the point. If I miss another one, he'll be crushed.

CAROL. Isn't your wife going?

GEORGE. Yes.

MARIE. Well, there you go. She can record it on her phone or whatever and you can watch it when you get back.

GEORGE. No, it's not the same. A boy needs to look up into the stands and see his father. You wouldn't understand because you don't have-- Wait a minute. Yeah, Marie, you don't have kids. *You* should go.

MARIE. Ooh, guys. I didn't want to say anything before, but ...

GEORGE. Yes?

MARIE. My husband just lost his job.

CAROL. Again?

MARIE. And he's started drinking.

GEORGE. What else is new?

MARIE. So that week, the whole family is coming into town for an intervention.

GEORGE. Oh, that's perfect! If the whole family will be there, you can take off for a week.

CAROL. Yeah, you don't want to be there for that mess.

MARIE. I can't just leave him at a time like this.

GEORGE. Ever think that maybe he drinks 'cause you're there?

MARIE. That's mean, George.

CAROL. Wait, I have the perfect solution ... pack him a bottle and take him with you.

MARIE. What?!

GEORGE. Ooh, that's great! He won't even know where he is. He'll think he's in the Bahamas or something!

MARIE. That is horrible. I can't believe you would even suggest something like that, Carol. You have no idea what it's like to be mar-- hey, wait a minute. Carol, *you're* not married. *You* should go.

GEORGE. That's right, Carol. No husband, no kids, no one to care for, no one who cares about you ...

CAROL. No way. You're not pushing this off on me.

MARIE. Why not?

CAROL. You guys know that I've been rehearsing for months and that's the week of my big dance recital.

GEORGE & MARIE. *Dance recital?!*

GEORGE. That's a hobby!

MARIE. Exactly. Is *that* your job or is *this* your job?

GEORGE. That would be like me saying I can't go because I need to work on my stamp collection.

CAROL. Now wait a minute--

MARIE. Hey, George? I won't be in next week because of my Monopoly tournament.

CAROL. My dancing is very important to me. I didn't go to Julliard for nothing.

GEORGE. Well, apparently you did, because you work *here*.

CAROL. If anyone's backing out for something trivial, George, it's you and your *soccer game*.

MARIE. That's right, Carol. George, you really need to be the one to go.

GEORGE. No way, guys. There is *no way* that I can look into my son's face and disappoint him.

CAROL. I've seen your son's face. It's already disappointing.

GEORGE. Well, not as disappointing as your "dancing," Carol.

MARIE. Okay, guys--

GEORGE. Or your drunk husband, Marie ...

(*The three continue arguing indefinitely.*)

***

In the real world, one would hope that decisions aren't made this way.

Oftentimes, at the end of this scene, we'll ask the audience to vote for who *they* think should fly. Unfortunately for poor Carol, she's usually the one sent packing (though George will usually score a couple votes because people just don't like him by program's end). The hierarchy in voting tends to be that kids come first and drunk husbands second, with personal and artistic fulfillment a distant third.

The point, of course, is that nobody's right and nobody's wrong. Each character has a valid reason for wanting to stay behind and each person's reason is equally important *to them*. They may resort to some pretty low tactics and the argument may get a bit heated, but they all have the same underlying motivation. Nobody is the villain.

We all see the world from our own point of view. Most tensions in the workplace occur when that point of view becomes too narrow and we fail to see the impact that our words and actions can have on others. But if we can keep our eyes open to the underlying motivations of our own behavior and the behavior of others, then we'll have a foundation from which to build a culture of respect in the workplace.

III

CONCLUSION

There's an inherent conceit in using drama to illustrate workplace issues. By depicting fictional situations, the writer can control the narrative and ultimately bend the lesson wherever he or she wants it to go. But it's important to note that the mini-dramas included here were not created out of whole cloth. Each scene came out of consultation with an HR professional who was seeing these situations being played out in their organization. Dramatizing these situations is not just a way to teach a lesson or entertain an audience. It's a way of getting to the heart of what drives people to behave the way they do. There are a million different ways these scenarios could play out in real life depending on the character of the people involved, the existing culture in the workplace and countless other variables. But while specific circumstances change, human nature is a constant, and theater artists have been exploring that nature ever since the first actors stepped onto the stage in ancient Greece over two thousand years ago.

It's doubtful that the scenes you've just read will stand with the works of Aeschylus, Shakespeare or Tennessee Williams two thousand years from now, and I'm quite okay with that. My ambition with this book is smaller. And with that, I'll close with a few brief thoughts.

If you've learned something in reading this that you didn't know before, I think that's great. If you're a trainer or an HR professional and this book has given you some ideas of what to do with your own training programs, I say run with them (not with *my* ideas, per se, but your own). But on a more personal note, I hope this book can make a difference, however minimal. Perhaps that won't happen on its own merits, but it might happen with you, the reader. If reading this has inspired you in even the smallest measure to be a little more mindful as you make your way through the workday, and to consider the value in someone else's point of view, then maybe *you* will be the difference. That might be corny, but I can't ignore the possibility that it might also be true. At any rate, I hope that you've enjoyed reading this book as much as I've enjoyed writing it. Be good to yourself.

And if you get a chance, go see a play sometime.

ABOUT THE AUTHOR

Geoffrey Scheer is the Managing Director of Access Communications, a corporate training firm created by Art Feinglass that uses theater, drama and no small amount of humor to train companies on a variety of subjects including discrimination, harassment and challenges to leadership. Prior to turning his attention to corporate America, Geoffrey spent fifteen years in New York working as an actor, singer, director, playwright and producer.

He is a contributing writer for TheHumanist.com and the author of numerous plays including *The Ex* (published by Samuel French © 2006), *After the Ball, Never Open the Mini-Bar* and the New York Times reviewed *On the Eighth Day*.

www.access-communications.com
Twitter: @scheer_geoffrey

www.ingramcontent.com/pod-product-compliance
Lightning Source LLC
Chambersburg PA
CBHW071043240526
45471CB00014B/474